Student Letting

The Professional Landlord's Guide To Buying & Renting Out Property

By

Simon Thompson

Student Letting

Published by: Simon Thompson c/o The Old Church, Albert Hill Street, Didsbury, Manchester M20 6RF

Email: support@accommodationforstudents.com
Visit my website at http://www.accommodationforstudents.com

Limited Liability/Disclaimer of Warranty

British Library Cataloguing in Publication Data: A catalogue record for this book is available from the British Library.

ISBN: 978-0-9573090-0-5

About the Author

Simon Thompson (pictured) set up the award-winning accommodationforstudents.com website in 2000, after experiencing difficulties in finding somewhere to live while a student.

Simon has developed the business into the leading UK student accommodation website, attracting around 3 million visits from students every year.

Among the numerous awards he has won, Simon was recognised in 2011 by North West Business Insider as one of the region's most influential young businesspeople in their annual '40 under 40' awards.

In 2005, Simon Thompson and his business partner, William Berry, turned down a substantial investment on BBC TV's Dragons Den.

Always striving for innovation, accommodationforstudents.com has partnered Unipol student homes to launch a national accreditation programme for student property aiming to improve housing standards.

Alongside accommodationforstudents.com, Simon owns a portfolio of web-based businesses, including Conferences Group, a successful conferencing and venue-finding service. He also offers digital marketing, search engine optimisation and web development consultancy to other businesses, and aids young entrepreneurs establishing their own enterprises.

Simon lives in the North West of England with his partner and young son, and works out of a converted church in South Manchester.

Quick Glance Inside

Introduction   1

Part 1: Student Letting - Facts & Figures   5

Chapter 1: Why Student Letting?   7
Chapter 2: Picking The Right Rental Property   17
Chapter 3: Avoiding An HMO Horror   34
Chapter 4: Getting Ready For Rental   44

Part 2: Dealing With Tenants   57

Chapter 5: Marketing A Student Let   59
Chapter 6: How To Screen Your Tenants   71
Chapter 7: During A Tenancy   85
Chapter 8: Ending A Tenancy   93

Part 3: Looking After The Finances   99

Chapter 9: All About Property Tax   101

Appendix A: University Cities   114
Appendix B: Student Landlord Toolkit   123
Appendix C: Online Resources   137

Contents

Introduction   **1**

About this book
Conventions Used In This Book
About You
Finding What You Need To Know
    Part 1 Student Letting - Facts and Figures
    Part 2 Dealing With Tenants
    Part 3 Looking After The Finances

Part 1: Student Letting - Facts & Figures   **5**

Chapter 1: Why Student Letting?   **7**

Crunching The Numbers   8
Britain's Top University Towns & Cities   12
Why Student Lets Top Other Property Investments   13
Different Kinds Of Investment   14
UK's Largest Student Landlord   15

Chapter 2: Picking The Right Rental Property   **17**

Focus On Your Property X Factor   18

Finding A Student Let   23
Figuring Out If An Investment Stacks Up   27
Tax-Effective Property Ownership   30
Taxes Affected By Income Shifting   32

Chapter 3: Avoiding HMO Horrors   **34**

What Is An HMO?   34
HMO Planning Permission   36
Licensing HMOs   39
HMO Licence Conditions   40

Chapter 4: Getting Ready For Rental   **44**

Timing Your Student Let   45
Permission To Let   45
Who Runs The Business?   46
Protecting Your Cash From Crooks   48
Landlord Insurance   51
Council Tax   53
Finish & Furnishings   53
Landlord Obligations & Duties   54

Part 2: Dealing With Tenants   *57*

Chapter 5: Marketing A Student Let   **59**

Accreditation Where It's Due   59
Setting The Rent   60
Finding The Right Tenants   64
Playing Your Calling Cards Right   65
Countdown For Viewing Checklist   67
Rooms With A View   68
Showing Off Your Property   68

Why You Need A Rental Application Form   69
Holding A Deposit   70

Chapter 6: Starting A Tenancy   71

How To Screen Your Tenants   72
Stamp Out Discrimination   72
Checking A Tenant's Credit History   74
Understanding Tenancy Agreements   74
Necessity Is The Mother Of Inventories   78
10 Tips For A Perfect Inventory   79
Protecting Deposits For Tenants   80
Consider A Property Guide   82

Chapter 7: During A Tenancy   85

Keep Those Rents Rolling In   86
Dealing With Repairs & Complaints   88
Visiting A Rental Property   90
Looking Out For Human Rights   90
Problem Tenants   91
Unlawful Evictions   92

Chapter 8: Ending A Tenancy   93

Getting Ready For Move-Out Day   94
Checking The Property   94
Special Move-Out Circumstances   96
Viewings Before A Tenant Moves Out   97
Watch Out For The Insurance Trap   97

Part 3: Looking After The Finances   99

Chapter 9: All About Property Tax   101

Understanding Property Tax 102
Who Pays Property Tax? 102
Tax & A Typical Landlord 103
When Is Property Tax Paid? 104
Telling The Tax Man About Income Tax 105
Telling The Tax Man About Capital Gains Tax 106
Accounting For Pre-Letting Expenses 106
Keeping A Property Register 107
Tagging Financial Records 109
Keeping Good Financial Records 110
Allocating Rent & Expenses To Tax Years 111
Dealing With Rental Losses 113
How Long Do You Keep The Records? 113

Appendix A: University Cities **114**

Appendix B: Student Landlord Toolkit **123**

Telephone Card 125
Viewing Card 126
Rental Application 127
Assigning & Releasing Deposits 131
Accounting For Deposits 132
Tenancy Agreement Violation Letter 134
Tenant's Notice To Vacate 135

Appendix C: Online Resources **137**

Introduction

· ·

A property business is just that - a business. All the general rules of running and marketing a business apply to student landlords as much as they do to British Airways or the local corner shop.

The key to a successful business is understanding your customers and providing them with the right products and services at a reasonable price. Student letting is about providing decent property in the right location at the right rent.

It's as simple as that, although success may seem easy once you are there. Every overnight sensation takes a lot of hard work, and running a successful letting business is no different.

Running a successful student letting business offers no easy way to riches. Student landlords work long hours sourcing, renovating and maintaining their property. After hours, someone needs to keep up with ever-changing letting laws and complete the accounts and tax returns.

This book is here to help you draw on the author's 12 years' experience in student letting and his feedback from countless landlords about their frustrations, successes and failures in the business.

About This Book

Student Letting is an in-depth guide for landlords renting property to students. First, it will help you understand how to research your business and source the right property.

Then, it will explain the legal considerations for letting a house in multiple occupation - a shared house for three or more tenants sharing a kitchen or bathroom. Lastly, you can find out about running your student letting business.

In summary, the book covers:

- Picking the right student property for rental profit

- Handling house in multiple occupation (HMO) issues

- Finding student tenants

- Managing rents, repairs and tenants

- Getting rid of bad tenants

- Keeping good financial records

- Paying less landlord and property tax

Don't worry about reading the book from cover to cover - the contents have been specially formatted so you can dip in where you would like to read a particular section.

Conventions Used In This Book

To help you get to the content you want, we've worked hard to keep to a consistent format:

- Square bullets like this one mark lists of important information

- Bold text introduces new topics or expands the current topic, like:

This is a section head

This is a subheading

Pages with a grey background contain incidental information that gives some background or examples about the chapter subject matter - but don't worry, these are not vital if you are in a hurry and can easily be skipped and read later.

About You

You have read a lot about us, so here is some information we assumed about you that we kept in mind while writing this book:

- You are a student landlord, or are thinking about dipping your toe in the water - maybe because you are looking at a cost-effective way to help a son or daughter with accommodation during their time at university

- You are not a lawyer or accountant, so need some legal pointers about things like planning, HMO licensing and tax for landlords

- You don't have the time to research stuffy guidance written by councils or other organisations with an agenda

- You want bite-size nuggets of information that tell you exactly what you need to know - and then point you to an online resource for further information

Finding What You Need to Know

This book is divided into four parts. Each part is split into chapters dealing with specific topics, broken down into sections. The two tables of contents will help you find your way - the first gives the contents at a glance and the second includes the main subheadings within each chapter.

Here's what you will discover in each part:

Part 1 - Student Letting Facts & Figures

Skip the first chapter if you like - this part looks at the student letting market in numbers, but if you already have student property, the data may be interesting but not that vital, while new landlords may find the information helps them decide where to buy and why.

The other chapters look at choosing a student letting property, the legal requirements of letting a shared house and readying your property for letting.

Part 2 - Dealing With Tenants

This part deals with the nitty-gritty of finding and managing student tenants.

Part 3 - Dealing With The Finances

An in-depth look at keeping financial records and paying tax on rental profits.

The Appendices

The last section offers three appendices giving more detailed statistics about the student letting market, template business forms and letters, and finally, some online resources for further research.

Part 1
Student Letting: Facts And Figures

Chapter 1

Why Student Letting?

- **■ *Crunching the numbers***
- **■ *Britain's top university towns and cities***
- **■ *Why student lets top other property investments***
- **■ *Different types of investment***

So you want to be a student landlord and would like to know some more about starting a property business before you take the plunge? Many prospective student landlords see the pound signs clocking up rental profits, but often fail to see the downsides of running a property business. They dive right in without considering the pros and cons.

Many student landlords take on the responsibility of maintaining and managing their properties and, for them, the business often becomes a lifestyle choice as well as a source of income.

Before buying a property, every prospective student landlord should sit down and make some tough decisions – the first two are where to invest and who will take on the day-to-day management of the rental business.

Homing in on the right place to invest involves serious research - and to make the task easy, this chapter puts together the latest statistics about student numbers, house prices and rents. You still have to make the business decisions on buying and running a property - and don't forget the figures are averages, so you need to check they apply to where you want to invest.

Crunching The Numbers

Working out whether letting to students is financially viable comes down to some simple number crunching.

Take a buy-to-let landlord renting a three-bedroom house to a young family. At the time of writing, the average UK rent for a house is £687 per month, according to the monthly letting survey by LSL Property Services.

The figures come from analysing the firm's sales and properties for rent – and as one of the UK's largest chains of letting agents, the figures are reasonably reliable. Their letting agent brands include well-known names like Your Move and Reeds Rains.

Now, take that same buy-to-let and rent to three students at, say, £80 a week each for a bedroom and shared facilities. This will pay the landlord £240 a week or £1,040 per month, around double of letting the same property to a family.

If the house is a large three-bed with a kitchen-diner, dining room and sitting room downstairs, the owner may have scope to take in an extra student and increase income by another £80 a week, up to a potential £1,386 a month.

Renting to students is more profitable then other letting because the business model generates more income from a property than any other type of rental.

Making more money is a definite plus for student letting, but the cost of entry into the market is also more expensive. Student landlords have to outlay more money to prepare a property for rental to comply with tighter fire, health and safety rules.

Additionally, student lets need more hands-on management than buy-to-lets, as a house split into multiple lets needs more attention.

The student letting market is huge and expanding. According to the Higher Education Statistics Agency (HESA), just fewer than 2.5 million students registered with higher education institutions in 2011-12, and 435,000 of them were from the European Union or overseas. The figures have progressively increased over the past 10 years and demand is expected to hold up for some time to come – despite the changes to the funding structure of higher education.

England, Scotland and Wales have around 75 key university towns and cities – and these institutions only have accommodation for 27% of students that sign up for courses, which is around 675,000 beds.

That leaves 1.825 million students seeking a home during term-time.

Next, come the big corporate accommodation providers. The largest is Unite Group. Unite offers around 40,000 beds. In terms of the market, universities and corporate landlords have an estimated 30% share, leaving private landlords to take up the slack of 1.78 million students.

What's the market worth?

Assuming each student pays an average £80 a week rent for 40 weeks a year, that makes the student rental market in the UK worth around £5.6 billion to private landlords.

Looking at the size of the market and demand for places should have any prospective student landlord rubbing their hands in glee at the prospect of the profits to be made. The trouble is, business is rarely as easy as that. The student letting business has lots of positives, but other factors beyond the control of landlords affect the market as well.

More students looking to study

Two simple factors are driving the demand for places – demographics mean that the country has more people leaving school at aged 18 than ever before. These young adults have two places to go – work or further education. The sorry state of the economy languishing in the post-recession doldrums is just not generating enough jobs, so school leavers are opting to shelter in further education. The hope of many youngsters is that they can ride out the country's economic woes while gaining qualifications to help them better compete for jobs.

The UK jobs market is in a state of flux after the recession. Around 2.5 million people are chasing 600,000 vacancies.

With the abolition of the default retirement age in April 2011, figures suggest half of those who would normally retire at 65 years old will work on for up to five years.

The Department of Work and Pensions reckons this adds around 400,000 people who would have been forced into retirement at 65 who will now stay in the jobs market. The knock-on effect is fewer job openings will become available and more people will chase them, leveraging more youngsters into further education to improve their chances against older and more experienced workers.

Soaring costs may keep students at home

As some families tighten their belts as tuition fees and living costs increase, some have speculated that some students on more general degree courses may take the cheaper option of staying with mum and dad.

The reality is that for over a decade a proportion of students have chosen to live at home, but the majority 75% or so, are likely to move away from home to study. It is important to remember that students do not pay their tuition fees until they graduate.

Corporates pulling back to London and big cities

Corporates aim to attract more affluent students from home and abroad, and to build accommodation within easy reach of more established learning institutions. This reduces investment risk as these universities are likely to continue to have a big demand for places. Reining in corporate competition to the capital leaves the way open for private landlords to fill the accommodation voids in many lucrative student rental markets.

Not enough student halls

Universities do not invest in student halls, and even if they had the money in these times of government cuts and austerity, they could not build enough bed spaces fast enough to fulfil demand. In fact, many universities are actively divesting themselves of halls to corporations like Unite Group in order to save management and repair costs.

Government policy

Since the 1990s, the government has encouraged more school leavers to go into further education - including university degree courses. In only 2009, the government put cash behind their commitment by funding an extra 10,000 university places.

The increase in tuition fees in England from the start of the 2012 academic year – with the maximum rising from £6,000 a year to £9,000 – may well have some impact on numbers from within the UK, but is unlikely to quell demand from overseas.

Applications for university had increased by 3.5% on 2012 figures.

Increasing international student demand

The UK is seen as providing a first-class university education by the rest of the world. Students from overseas already make up 18% of the market.

Demand from overseas is just as insatiable as that from within the UK, so the likelihood is any downturn on UK student numbers is likely to be filled from abroad.

Changing planning policies

Many councils are under siege from residents complaining about the 'studenti-fication' of some neighbourhoods close to universities. These councils are taking on special planning controls to limit the number of shared houses for students in some neighbourhoods.

The government is considering a fast-track planning amnesty on converting disused commercial buildings into homes. Both these policies will have an impact on where a student landlord can site a rental property. *See Chapter 3 - Avoiding HMO Horrors* for more information about student house planning and licensing.

Britain's Top University Towns and Cities

London is the UK's biggest student letting market, with 40 leading higher educa-tion institutions offering courses to around 460,000 students from home and abroad.

TABLE 1: Top university cities by student numbers

City		Student population	Market share
1	London	460,830	21%
2	Manchester	96,685	4%
3	Birmingham	72,575	3%
4	Leeds	64,990	3%
5	Glasgow	64,790	3%
6	Nottingham	63,560	3%
7	Sheffield	63,125	3%
8	Cardiff	61,945	3%
9	Edinburgh	57,850	3%
10	Liverpool	54,780	2%

Source: HESA student enrolments 2012-13

TABLE 2: Student property average rents and yields

	Studio rent	En Suite rent	Rental change	Yield
London	£278	£210	8%	15%
Regional	£142	£102	4%	10.5%
England & Wales	£177.62	£112.18	2.17%	6.25%

Source: Student lettings review – Knight Frank September 2012

The capital takes 21% of the student market, dwarfing every other town and city. Manchester lags behind in second, with three universities and the Royal Northern College of Music, offering around 96,865 places to students, which equals 4% of the UK total.

For key data on the UK's university cities, see Appendix A: University Cities

Why Student Lets Top Other Property Investments

Student lettings led the way in property investment with increases in rents, property values and returns on investment in the past year. Overall, student landlords enjoyed a remarkable 15% return in a financial year characterised by poor economic performance in most other industry sectors.

The latest student property survey for England and Wales, by estate agents Knight Frank (September 2012), shows:

- ■ Average student rents rose by 6%

- ■ Average London rents rose by 8%, while rents for other university cities in England and Wales increased by 4%

- ■ Yields in London almost doubled - from 8% in 2011 to 15% in 2012, while those in the regions climbed around 4% to just over 10% - after a slight fall the year before

Where student lets outstrip other house prices

House price growth in student cities is outstripping increases in other locations by up to 65%, while rental yields can hit as high as 10%. The figures come from separate reports by Lloyds Bank and online property portal Globrix.

Both come to the conclusion that while student numbers are growing, accommodation is limited, as only one bed space was created for each eight new student places at a university in 2009 – and the student population is still set to grow.

The Lloyds data shows half of the UK's 72 student towns and cities had average house price increases that outstripped regional growth by up to 65%. Three student house price hotspots were Aberystwyth, Aberdeen and Winchester.

Globrix pinpoints Glasgow as another student investment hotspot – and properties there already show a 10% net yield. What's more, the city has no shortage of students looking for a place to live, as the city has a choice of three universities.

Another point to note is Scottish degrees last four years instead of three in England, giving a potential extra year of income for each student.

Different Kinds Of Investment

Investing in student accommodation comes in several different types -

- Direct ownership

- Active purchase, ownership and management of letting property

- Investing in corporates

- Buying shares in listed or unlisted companies, like Unite plc

- Investing in funds

The UK's largest student landlord

Understanding the student letting market means understanding a little about the country's largest student landlord – Unite.

The organisation runs a slick marketing machine linked to cost-effective and attractive all-in packages for students. However, although Unite operates student halls all over the UK offering thousands of beds, the core business is focused on London and the management have indicated that they intend to develop exclusively in the capital in the short-term.

The firm has spent millions on marketing and, as a public company, reveals a lot of corporate business thinking about student letting that is of interest to other landlords. They should know what they are talking about with student halls valued at £30 billion, offering 40,000 bed spaces to students at 50 universities.

Some of Unite's strategies do not translate well to a smaller student letting business – but two policy mainstays are worth considering any location with two or more further education institutions:

- Unite is moving away from tying accommodation to universities in favour of building near transport hubs. The key is to provide easy access to multiple places of learning. This increases demand for student beds and decreases reliance on the success of a single institution.

- Selling student accommodation as a package rather than just renting a room and leaving tenants to sort out the rest for themselves. Unite offers broadband, wi-fi, cable TV and all-inclusive letting deals bundled with utility bills and insurance.

Unite can negotiate discounts with suppliers and price as no-stress, no-hassle packages for youngsters moving away from home for the first time who may have apprehensions about striking out on their own.

■ From time to time, investment houses, banks and companies raise money for student developments by inviting investors to lend money over a fixed period of time in return for a guaranteed return.

Many of these investments are corporate bonds with a minimum buy-in value of at least £10,000 at 5% over five years.

That means that the investor receives £500 interest each year and £10,000 back at the end of the term. Different investors will have varied appetites for risk that will govern their choice of how to invest in student letting.

TABLE 3: University cities with the largest house price increases

	Average House Price 2001	Average House Price 2011	10-year Average House Price Change
Edinburgh	£194,943	£258,531	103%
Exeter	£101,313	£205,281	91%
Loughborough	£88,969	£169,871	90%
Cambridge	£154,826	£291,079	88%
Leicester	£79,006	£148,898	88%
Lancaster	£77,254	£142,331	84%
Sheffield	£70,229	£126,863	81%
Warwick	£76,159	£137,092	80%
St Andrews	£168,234	£299,606	78%
York	£101,096	£179,036	78%

Source: Lloyds Banking Group 2012

Chapter 2
Picking The Right Rental Property

● ●

- *Focus on your property X factor*
- *Finding a student let*
- *Figuring out if the investment stacks up*
- *Tax-effective property ownership*

● ●

Location, location, location is the catchphrase that comes to mind when looking for a home, and this is doubly important when trying to find the perfect student rental property. Sourcing student property can go against the grain for property investors who do not realise the needs of their market.

Students do not want the same from a property as a married couple or family. Nevertheless, a property investor has to bear in mind the same financial considerations, like buying a property that will appreciate in value over time and is the right type of home in the right location.

In Chapter 1, the emphasis was on the market - where do students study, how much rent do they pay and which university cities give the best property returns? In this chapter, attention switches to the property and how to identify the right home that is easily manageable while giving a good return on investment.

Focus On Your Property X Factor

Do you really think those X Factor judges sit through thousands of auditions from all those woeful hopefuls who can't sing a note? Of course they don't. They have a panel that pre-auditions the contestants and they only see the best of the bunch - mixed in with a few who are so awful they make us laugh.

Property investors need to adopt the same attitude to sourcing property to save time and money.

Every university city has thousands of properties on the market - most of which are totally unsuitable for student letting.

Sellers and estate agents are so desperate to shift property, they will bombard you with details of properties that will never make a good student let.

You need to weed out those turkeys so you don't waste time and money. The best way to do this is to score properties offered to you - and dump those that do not meet your pass mark.

Whatever anyone says, size does matter!

Students like to share in groups of generally three or more. Some student couples look for smaller homes, but they are a minor percentage of the market and any student landlord cut off from the mainstream demand to service a niche market is severely restricting the chances of running a profitable letting business.

The profitability of a student let is determined by the number of bed spaces.

The number of bed spaces relates to:

- Type of property

- Planning regulations that govern the letting of shared houses

The ideal student let sleeps at least three people, which puts many standard homes with three bedrooms in the frame.

Some older two-bedroom Victorian or Edwardian terraces have spacious rooms with high ceilings that convert easily into an extra bedroom to let a landlord maximise income by easily fitting in an extra tenant - see page 28 for an explanation of yields and how to calculate them.

The problem is some city councils are looking to contain the spread of shared housing with planning controls. These controls let councils dictate the number of tenants for a student let.

See HMO Planning Permission on Page 36 for more information about shared house planning permission.

Property that is too small can restrict a property business, but somewhere too big can also cause landlords a headache.

Homes on large plots with extensive lawns and never-ending fences are expensive to maintain. If you are a DIY landlord managing your own property, someone has to cut those acres of lawns. You can bet that won't be your student tenants.

Compact is better. A property with grounds and a number of bedrooms that reflects the price of neighbouring homes is better than somewhere over-extended on a tight plot, or a mansion sitting in rambling grounds.

Ironing out the costs of owning a flat

Flats often seem a sensible financial option, but they do come with drawbacks.

The freeholder will have to give permission to sublet, so you need a clause in the lease or a written waiver from the block owner to rent to tenants.

This agreement could come with restrictions about letting to tenants.

The running costs may seem cheaper, but flats are sometimes the more expensive option when service charges and ground rents are added in. Check the lease for the hidden costs of maintaining and upgrading the property.

Day-to-day expenses are generally covered in the service charge, the big repair costs like a new roof, painting the outside of the block or replacing the windows are not. These costs are generally calculated by taking the floor area of each flat as a percentage of the block's floor area and billing the leaseholders pro rata.

If your flat is 15% of the block's floor area, and the external repair bill is £35,000, your share of the cost is £5,250. Sometimes, the freeholder does not give you a say in who carries out the work or whether an alternative quote would be a cheaper option.

If flats have recently undergone refurbishment, you might not have to chip into the repair pot for several years, but be wary of a run down block.

Many professional property investors prefer to control their costs by buying freehold houses rather than leasehold flats.

Calculating your budget

Setting a budget determines the size and location of your property. Realistically, a property investor needs a deposit of 30% - 40% of a property's value to find a competitive mortgage interest rate.

Add to that a survey, legal costs and a mortgage arrangement fee of at least £1,000 and the extra expenses probably add up to more like 3% of the loan.

Don't forget to work pre-letting costs into the budget - these include financing the mortgage and bills until the first income starts rolling in; refurbishment and redecoration costs and fitting the house out with furniture.

All in all, the cost of entry into the student lettings market is relatively high and if you do not have enough cash available, ask yourself whether setting your sights lower might be more sensible.

This could mean buying a buy-to-let instead of a student let, or a joint venture with a business partner who could share the risk and the cost.

See Figuring Out If An Investment Stacks Up on Page 27 for more about finance.

Location, location, location

This is positively the last time you'll see the phrase in this book. Nevertheless, although the phrase is overused and often misinterpreted, property location is an important factor in any rental business.

All those tables and statistics in the previous chapter were aimed at giving a prospective student landlord the information for putting together a business plan. That business plan should include an explanation of why a specific property should work as a student let.

The smart money is pouring into student letting from corporate investors, and as a small private investor swimming in the same pool as the sharks, you might do well to look how they are spending.

The trend for student let development in cities with two or more universities is not to tie the property to an institution but to site accommodation close to a transport hub. This lets students from multiple learning centres live in the same property.

The key is landlords are not so dependent on decisions made by a university that can affect the letting market, like charging more for courses or reducing student numbers.

In general, students like to live in a neighbourhood with other students within easy distance or travel to campus and entertainment.

Remember your Plan B

It's easy to get caught up in the moment when investing in property, and not to think long-term. Property is a long-term investment, and that means a minimum of 10-15 years down the line.

But don't forget the what if: like what if you have to sell early for some unforeseen reason?

When choosing a property, factor a forced or quick sale into your calculations. That means not buying a home that no one else would want to buy. An average property in a nice location is better than a non-standard home in an odd location.

State of repair

Buying property that needs some tender love and care or a major refurbishment comes down to budget.

If the state of repair of a property significantly reduces the price, the time and money involved in reinstatement adds value, which makes the project worth considering.

Some property investors are builders by trade, so this kind of project is more suited to their skills. Others have problems changing a light bulb, so a big refurbishment would involve calling in tradespeople; which adds to the cost.

Some points to consider when looking at a rundown property are:

- ■ **Cost** - Depending on the repair of the building, a refurbishment may require more cash input than a property that needs redecoration.

- ■ **Added value** - Check out the likely value at the end of the project increases the property price. Show the plans to a valuer, not an estate agent, for a professional view.

- **Skills** - Managing a building project can be a daunting task, especially if you are coping with a family and a day job

- **Downtime** - How long will a refurbishment take and will you miss the student letting window for the next academic year?

Finding A Student Let

Finding property is not the problem. Plenty of sellers and agents with pound signs in their eyes are only too pleased to find you that right property - for a price.

Work with them, because they might come up with the perfect student let, but do not let them sway you from choosing the property you want within the budget you have set. All you have to do now is decide whether to stay local or look further afield.

Location, location, location - part 2

OK, so I did say I would not wheel out that phrase again, but once a property investor has decided to put money into a student let, the next decision is where to buy.

As an investor, you may already live in a university city. That could make the decision easier - if the local market is saturated with student landlords and corporate halls, then joining the frenzy to find tenants might not be a good idea.

If your city has an under supply of accommodation, then the way is clear to go ahead. Budget may restrict investment choice.

The pound in your wallet might stretch a good deal further in a northern university city than in London or the Home Counties.

Long-distance property investment is strongly reliant on agents and other third parties. Managing a refurbishment, out-of-term maintenance and general administration becomes a lot harder and costs more the further you live from your property.

Grouping student lets or other investment properties close to home lets you benefit from economies of scale, and that quick inspection is not a three-day trip.

Hopefully, by now you have enough information at your fingertips to decide where to look for your student let, so it's a matter of zooming in on the area to see what is for sale.

Searching the web

The internet has opened up a world of possibilities for property investors but, although access to homes for sale is quick and easy, generally it is more of the same as property ads are copied and recopied between media. With more than 30 popular web portals and thousands of estate agent websites, searching the internet can take as much time as you want to spend.

Here's a handy list of major property websites to save time:

- **Rightmove** (www.rightmove.co.uk) is the portal listing the most property and picks up the most page views

- **Other web portals** include Student Accommodation For Sale (www.studentaccommodationforsale.com), Globrix (www.globrix.com), Zoopla (www.zoopla.co.uk) and findaproperty (www.findaproperty.com)

These sites cover around 90% or more of property for sale in the UK.

Dealing with estate agents

Don't let the sharp suits and sales spiel fool you. Most estate agents know little or nothing about your property business. Estate agents are sales people working for the seller.

They want to shift property on their books to earn commission and see you as a prospect to convert to a customer.

At some point in the vast majority of sales, you will have to deal with an estate agent to make viewing appointments and negotiate the buying price. Do not disclose your hand to them.

Watch out for the older, more experienced estate agents who are knowledgeable about their area and can offer genuine insight that could help your property business. The trouble is, these are few and far between.

Tracking the local press

Reading local papers probably won't help you find a property - they are mostly online anyway, but you can pick up information about an area.

Try scanning the paper's website for 'student' or the local university for useful information; like plans to expand the number of courses, planning issues and noisy-neighbour disputes.

Hammering home the point about auctions

Most property investors think about buying at auction at some time, but this is a bear pit where you need to fight for survival.

Yes, auctions can present some property bargains, but always think about why a property is at auction. The two main reasons are the property is defective or a repossession that can't be sold by an estate agent.

A defective home is generally not mortgagable, so presents problems over financing that can make the deal expensive and stressful.

Alarm bells should also start ringing if a home doesn't sell through the normal channels. If you do buy at an auction, bear in mind these three tips:

- Thoroughly check out any property you intend to bid on. Look for structural defects and issues in the title, so team up with a builder and a lawyer before the auction.

- Arrange your finance in advance. Most auction purchases require a 10% deposit when the hammer goes down, with the rest due no more than 28 days later. Buyers that can't complete could lose their deposit.

- Many property professionals have a bridging loan to secure the deal and remortgage to get their money back after refurbishment.

Sourcing below market value leads

Property-sourcing firms are a comparatively new way to take the pain out of finding homes to let. Property sourcers work in a similar way to estate agents, but purport to find 'below market value' or 'BMV' homes that they package as investment deals.

These firms work with homeowners who are desperate to sell and try to arrange a buying price of 30% BMV. The property sourcer then charges the buyer a fee for the sales lead. These fees can add up to several thousand pounds.

The leads are generally exclusive private sales.

Property sourcing is a grey area. The transaction is perfectly legal, but the sellers are prone to drop out as they have no commitment to a deal, are often in severe financial difficulties and may face repossession.

Some investors have built large portfolios quickly by working with property sourcers; others have not had such good experiences and have lost substantial amounts of money to fraudsters and badly-run businesses.

Property sourcers are not regulated, so fees and deposits handed to them are not protected.

Figuring Out If An Investment Stacks Up

A property deal that stacks up is one where the finances show a potential profit.

Three simple calculations are good indicators of whether a property is worth pursuing.

Rental yield

Yield is the financial return on capital invested. The formula is expressed as a percentage, and the higher the percentage, the better the return on investment.

Back on Page 13, Table 2 shows the average yields for student lets in England and Wales as 8%.

That is the benchmark - a property yielding less is underperforming and one offering more is outstripping the market. Follow these steps to calculate rental yield:

- Take the annual rental income

- Add up the annual business expenses, like insurance, repairs and loan interest

- Subtract expenses from income to give a net profit

- Add up your cash investment in the property - that's the deposit and annual expenses (from step 2 above)

- Divide the profit or loss (from step 3 above) by your cash investment

- Multiply by 100 to give a percentage

For example, you buy a student letting house for £165,000. The deposit was £49,500 and the rental income is £13,340 a year.

■ Rental income = £13,340

■ Business expenses = £7,500

■ Net profit = £5,840

■ Cash investment = £57,000

■ Divide profit by investment = 5,840/57,000 = 0.102

■ Yield = 0.102 x 100 = 10.2%

Rent cover

Most banks and building societies lending to property investors stipulate rent cover in their calculation for working out maximum borrowing levels. For example, rent cover of 125% means the monthly rent should clear the monthly interest -only mortgage repayment by 25%. The interest rate varies between lenders, but is generally 5%.

In our example of rental yield, the rent cover on borrowing of £115,500 at 5% interest needs to be £481 a month. The rental income is £1,111 per month.

The formula is (Mortgage x Interest Rate%)/12.

If the monthly rental is less than the rent cover, the lender will reduce any advance. For example, if the rent is £425 a month, maximum borrowing would work out as £81,600:

■ Reduce the rent to 100% of the mortgage repayment: £425/5 x 4 = £340
■ Work out the monthly mortgage interest: £340 x 12 = £4,080
    Round up the mortgage interest to the amount borrowed: (£4080/5) x 100 = £81,600

Regardless of the maximum loan-to-value on a property investment mortgage, the actual borrowing is always limited to the rent cover.

Loan-to-value

Loan-to-value is the amount a mortgage lender will advance against the purchase price of a property.

The trick in the tail is the mortgage offer will have a clause along the lines of 'the maximum loan to value is 75% of the purchase price or valuation, whichever is the lowest'.

That means you can agree any purchase price you like, but the mortgage will be based on the surveyor's valuation.

Calculating an affordable property from your deposit

You can benchmark the rent cover and loan-to-value you need by working backwards from the cash you have as a deposit. This test shows if you can afford a property. For example, you have £90,000 available to buy and prepare a property as a student let. From that £90,000, you will have to pay:

- A cash deposit of around 30% loan-to value of the property price

- Buying costs, including stamp duty and legal fees, say £5,000

- Lender's arrangement fee of around £1,000 - but this can be added to the loan without affecting the borrowing

- Refurbishment costs, budget another £5,000

- Furnishing costs, say £3,000

- Cash reserve for unforeseen costs, say £5,000

- Running costs until the property is let, say £3,500 to cover six months without rent

All that adds up to £22,500 with the option of setting off the lender's arrangement fee to the loan. That leaves £67,500 as a deposit from our original £90,000.

If £90,000 is 30% of the property value, then the maximum property price you can pay is £90,000/30 x 100 = £300,000

The formula is: (Deposit/Loan-to-value x 100) x 100

Stacking up the investment

These four formulae are the stress-test calculations property professionals and mortgage underwriters run to test whether your property deal stacks up within the terms and conditions of the loan.

To stack up a property investment, you must know the market price of a property and the likely rental return.

If you don't, you can easily put offers in on property where the finances fail to support the borrowing. The option then is to find a large deposit to make up the mortgage shortfall or pull out and look for somewhere else.

The rent cover and loan-to-value tests should be applied to every property before viewing to cut out deals that won't stack up.

Tax-Effective Property Ownership

Tax planning is often a last gasp consideration, but should start at the time of buying a property.

For individuals, the options are sole purchaser, buying as joint tenants or tenants in common.

When considering the best tax-effective ownership for a property, always look at the bigger picture and how your decision will impact other tax issues.

Under English law, a property can have up to four joint owners.

The guidance here is general information, but always take independent advice from an accountant before instructing your solicitor on how to proceed with the conveyancing.

Deciding how to split property ownership at the start is cheaper than having to revisit the decision in later years, as the cost is part of the conveyancing.

Sole ownership

If you are buying the property on your own, you do not have much choice about setting up ownership - you are the sole owner, so any rental profits or capital gains belong to you for tax.

Joint tenants

Each owner has an equal share of the property in a joint tenancy. The percentage cannot change, so two owners have 50% shares, three 33% shares and four 25% shares.

Tenants in common

If the owners do not allocate specific shares, then the default is equal shares, like joint tenants.

Owners can split the share of a property how they wish, so four owners could own a property 1%:1%:1%:97%.

Owning a property as tenants in common lets the owners income shift to save tax.

For unmarried partners, fixing the shares of ownership on buying a property beats capital gains tax, because switching later could trigger a demand for cash from the tax man.

For married partners, transfers of all or part of a property is exempt from capital gains tax, so the percentages can be set when necessary to cut tax bills.

A point to watch when switching shares in a property is stamp duty. If a property is mortgaged and equity is shuffled, then stamp duty might be due if the value of the share is over the stamp duty threshold.

Taxes Affected By Income Shifting

Making a decision to alter the ownership of a property can have extensive tax repercussions that might not come to light for many years. Here's a list of the major taxes that may change when income is shifted:

Income tax

Each taxpayer splits rental profits or losses pro rata their share of ownership, so if a property makes a £5,000 rental profit and is owned 50:50 by a couple; each pays income tax at their highest rate on 50% of the profits - in this case £2,500.

For a 40% taxpayer, that's £1,000, while a 20% taxpayer would pay £500. Income shifting is easily demonstrated by altering the ownership shares to 80:20 in favour of the lower rate taxpayer.

Now, the tax at 40% is £400 on £1,000, while the 20% taxpayer has a bill of £800 on £4,000. Shifting the shares has reduced the tax bill from £1,500 to £1,200 on the same profits.

Capital gains tax

Income shifting also impacts on capital gains tax (CGT). If our couple sold their rental property for a gain of £60,000 after reliefs and allowances, as 50:50 partners the tax would be £8,400 at 28% on £30,000 for the higher rate taxpayer, while the lower rate partner would pay £5,400 at 18% on their £30,000 share.

That's a total CGT bill of £13,800. But that 80:20 split applies to CGT as well as income tax, so the adjusted calculation is £3,360 for the higher rate taxpayer and £8,640 for the other partner, making a total CGT bill of £12,000.

Chapter 3
Avoiding HMO Horrors

● ●

- *What is an HMO?*
- *HMO planning permission*
- *Licensing HMOs*
- *Applying for an HMO licence*

● ●

Student landlords have a heap of bureaucracy that governs the running of their shared houses because they come under planning and licensing controls for a class of residential property termed 'houses in multiple occupation' or 'HMOs'.

Property investors are tied up in HMO red tape as a result of the government deciding to try and raise housing standards in substandard bedsit accommodation.

The term HMO was introduced in the Housing Act 2004 with subsequent modifications in other statutes and statutory instruments. This chapter looks at HMO rules in more detail.

What Is An HMO?

An HMO is simply a home with one front door where the tenants have to leave their own living space to share amenities like kitchens and bathrooms. The planning superhighway has three lanes for shared houses - two sets of rules for small HMOs and a single set of rules for large HMOs.

Note that these rules apply only to HMOs in England. Scotland and Wales have their own HMO planning guidelines that are similar, but not necessarily the same. To make sure you are working to the right set of rules, consult a planning specialist or the local council where the property is located.

The added complication to planning rules comes from a tacked-on piece of legislation termed an 'article 4 direction. This refers to powers local councils can take on under the Town and Country Planning (General Permitted Development) Order 1995.

For student landlords, these powers mean any new HMOs in areas where an article 4 direction applies must go to planning and receive consent before letting.

Councils wield this power to restrict the number of HMOs in a neighbourhood and to enforce housing standards.

Article 4 directions apply only to small HMOs, giving a slow and fast lane on our planning superhighway for these homes.

Small HMOs

A small HMO is a house or flat where three to five unrelated individuals share amenities, like a kitchen or bathroom.

Students who live in the property all year are considered as living in the property as their home, even if they live elsewhere out of term. A small HMO is determined by the number of people living in the property, not by any conversion or adaptation.

- **Small HMO slow lane** - Neighbourhoods where property investors must apply for planning permission

- **Small HMO fast lane** - Neighbourhoods where no planning permission is needed

No official central list of councils who have applied for article 4 directions is available. The only way to find out if a property needs planning permission is to ask the council. The planning issue creates a dilemma for property investors wanting to open a new small HMO as the council will not guarantee granting permission before reviewing an application. This can take weeks in some cities.

This uncertainty stops investors completing purchases because, if they buy a property without planning, it's a lottery whether permission is granted.

No sensible property investor should invest significant sums of money in buying and readying a property to let without written planning permission.

Large HMOs

A large HMO is a house or flat where six or more unrelated people live and share amenities. These properties always need planning permission.

Landlords taking in lodgers

If you own or rent your own home and take in two lodgers, the property does not become a HMO and no permissions or licences are needed.

Taking in a third lodger changes the game - the property may become a small HMO as three unrelated people share basic amenities.

HMO Planning Permission

HMOs need planning permission under two circumstances:

■ The property is a large HMO

■ The property is a small HMO in a neighbourhood subject to an article 4 direction

The problem with article 4 planning permission is an investor in small HMOs cannot complete a property purchase without consent in place. Without full consent, the investor runs the risk of locking capital in a property that can only trade as a buy-to-let, stifling cash flow and profits.

In the short-term, councils with Article 4 declarations to control HMO development are blighting neighbourhoods by pushing down property prices because the stimulation of investment potential is removed.

The issue has little effect on large HMOs as they need planning permission anyway.

Obtaining planning approval can end up a lottery, especially if the application attracts protests from residents. The application also costs an investor time and money, including the cost of detailed drawings to support the proposal and a fee to the local council.

Applications can easily take two to three months to reach the decision stage. In this time, the deal can easily go cold as sellers drop out.

When does a small HMO need planning?

A small HMO only needs planning if the council has taken on article 4 powers under the Town and Country Planning (General Permitted Development) Order 1995 and three to five unrelated tenants are sharing the kitchen and/or bathroom.

- ■ If the home was already a small HMO before the council took on the article 4 power, the property can continue as a HMO without planning permission, but might need a licence from the council.

- ■ If the home was let as a small HMO before the council took on article 4 powers, changes back to a standard buy-to-let and then the landlord wants to switch back to letting as a small HMO, planning permission is needed.

If the home is in a council area with no article 4 powers, planning permission is not needed for a small HMO.

Does a small HMO ever need planning permission?

Planning law is complicated. Effectively, the issue revolves around change of use of a residential property.

A standard family home is a Class C3 property, and a small HMO is Class C4.

Owners can shift the use between the two classes under a permitted development order, which is simply a rule that cuts red tape by doing away with the need for planning approval.

Councils can bypass this rule by applying an article 4 direction, which calls for planning approval for a material change of use.

However, a property investor could argue that moving a property from Class C3 to Class C4 is not a material change of use but permitted development, which negates the need for planning approval.

This view is supported in law by a planning inspector in a case in March 2010.

The decision involved changing the use of a family home to a five-bed HMO in Bolton.

The council rejected the plan on the grounds that the noise from the tenants would be detrimental to the neighbours and the area.

The planning inspector disagreed, pointing out that the HMO would be unlikely to generate more noise than a family of five living at the same house.

The full decision is available for download from http://painsmith.files.wordpress.com/2010/08/albertrddecision.pdf

Licensing HMOs

Many HMO owners confuse planning with licensing. They are separate issues and although large HMOs always require planning and licensing, many small HMOs may not.

Licensing has three aims:

■ Ensuring the HMO manager is a 'fit and proper' person

■ The property is managed according to health and safety standards

■ The HMO is not overcrowded

A point to watch is mandatory licensing for a small HMO. Even if a property is a small HMO because the tenants number five or less, if the living space stretches over three floors, the property still needs a mandatory licence, the same as a HMO for six or more tenants.

Mandatory licensing

Mandatory licensing applies to an HMO where the property:

■ Has three or more storeys

■ Is lived in by five or more persons

■ Is made up of two or more households

Selective or additional HMO licensing

Councils have the discretion to designate some or all of their neighbourhoods for selective or additional licensing, which are the same. Selective licensing lets councils apply licensing controls to small HMOs.

To apply the licensing controls, the council has to show:

■ The area has problems arising from poor HMO management

■ Other action to control the problems is not available

■ Selective licensing is consistent with the council's housing strategy

■ The views of residents and landlords in the neighbourhood have been canvassed

Once in place, the HMO owner has to apply for a licence, which can come with specific conditions relating to the neighbourhood.

Licensing responsibility

The HMO owner has the responsibility of applying for a licence, regardless of whether the council requests an application. Failing to licence an HMO is an offence punishable by a fine.

Besides fines and costs for breaching licensing regulations, councils and tenants can also take offending landlords to a rents tribunal, where an order to repay rents can be made for up to a 12-month period leading up to the date the offence was uncovered.

HMO Licence Conditions

A council has to grant an HMO licence, providing certain criteria are met:

■ The property is reasonably suitable for the number of tenants designated under the licence

■ The manager is a fit and proper person - the manager is the owner, a third party or a letting agent

- The licensee is the most appropriate person to hold the licence

- Proposals for managing the property meet council approval

- The HMO manager is competent

Fit and proper person

The main factors considered under the fit and proper person test are:

- **Convictions** - for violence, sexual offences, drugs and fraud

- **Landlord track record** - especially of breaching landlord/tenant law

- **Discrimination** - this covers any Equality Act 2010 convictions

Licence conditions

All mandatory and selective licensees will specify the number of tenants allowed to live in an HMO. There are also general conditions to every licence:

- A valid gas safety certificate must be provided

- Valid safety test certificates for electrical appliances must be provided

- Smoke alarms and emergency lights should be installed

- Tenants must have a written licence to occupy or a tenancy agreement

Councils can also apply other conditions that may include:

- Restricting property use

- Keeping the property in good repair

Duties of HMO managers

HMO regulations put a special burden on the manager of a shared house - often this is the property owner or landlord, but an employee or letting agent can take on the task.

HMO owners delegating shared house management to letting agents should make sure they have a clear agreement specifying responsibility for the various duties of the manager.

Don't forget this manager also has to pass the 'fit and proper person' test, so check out their credentials before handing over the reins. One specific problem area is councils do not keep a central register of 'fit and proper' people - or those that are not.

Some London councils are working together on a joint database, but referencing third-party credentials is still a little hit-and-miss.

The responsibilities of an HMO manager are laid out in the Management of Houses In Multiple Occupation (England) Regulations 2006. Many of them apply to Wales and Scotland, but each regional assembly has their own rules as well. Breaking the regulations is a criminal offence, with a maximum fine of £5,000.

Here are some of the more important points the manager must watch:

■ The manager's name, address and contact number must be given to all tenants and a notice carrying the same information must be prominently displayed in the common area of a shared house.

■ Fire escape routes must be clear and alarms, fire-fighting equipment and emergency lighting should work. In shared houses with five or more tenants, signs explaining what to do in a fire should be clearly displayed.

■ Gas and electricity - gas supplies and appliances should be tested by a qualified engineer at least once a year and a safety certificate supplied to the council. Electrical fittings should be tested every five years.

■ Common parts, like shared living space, halls, stairs and landings, should be kept clean, unobstructed and in good decorative order.

■ The manager should carry out a fire risk assessment and should take any action required to minimise the risk of fire in common areas.

Duties of HMO tenants

Much is said about the duties and responsibilities of shared house landlords, but the law also places obligations on tenants - and if they flout the rules, they could face prosecution as well. Tenants must:

■ Let the manager into their living space at any reasonable time to carry out repairs etc

■ Not carelessly cause damage

■ Dispose of litter as directed

■ Comply with fire safety instructions

Chapter 4
Getting Ready For Rental

- *Timing your student let*
- *Who runs the business?*
- *Protecting your cash from crooks*
- *Landlord obligations and duties*

How complicated can getting a property ready to let really be? Most landlords, especially those running houses in multiple occupation (HMOs), have lists of basic tasks they have to consider. These range from preparing the home, to checking out a landlord's legal obligations - of which there are many.

This chapter is a guide to preparing a buy-to-let or HMO to a state of readiness for viewing by tenants.

New landlords can find out about some of the finer legal points that they might otherwise overlook, while more experienced landlords can brush up on their skills. Landlord and tenant law is constantly changing - and some rules relate only to HMOs, while others are specific to England, Wales or Scotland.

The best way to check which rules apply is to contact the housing department of the local council for the area where the property is located.

Beware because council guidance is their interpretation of the law and, is not necessarily the final word, which is based on a judge in court.

Timing Your Student Let

Student lets revolve around their own calendar and the academic year, which runs from September through to July. The peak viewing times are January to March. Summer is a quiet time as most first-year students like to move into university halls.

Universities also hold housing fairs in January or February for prospective students. It's sensible to time buying and preparing a property to let around these dates.

For many projects, buying around March or April with a view to have the property on the market for the end of May and let from September is a good timetable.

This reduces downtime for the landlord - bringing a property online in January could mean the landlord having to put significant extra working capital aside to pay the bills.

Permission To Let

Landlords who have a mortgage or a leasehold title to a property may need permission to let from their lender or landlord.

Buy-to-let mortgages will come with implied permission that the property will be let to tenants, but if you are a let-to-buy investor moving out of your own home and letting, you should check your lender's terms before moving in tenants.

They could charge you a fee for granting permission and often hike the mortgage rate in line with buy-to-let rates. Any property owner who has a mortgage or is not a freeholder may need to secure the necessary permissions before they let the property.

Leaseholders will undoubtedly have a clause in their agreement warning against subletting. Apply to the freeholder in writing for permission to sublet. The freeholder cannot reasonably refuse, but may insist on an agreement limiting the number of tenants and how to deal with complaints, noise, parking and rubbish.

Without this permission, letting breaks the terms of the lease and, in extreme cases, could lead to eviction.

Who Runs The Business?

Letting student property or any other type of multiple let can return higher profits than other residential property letting, but there's no gain without some pain. In the case of student landlords, this pain is the extra time and stress involved in managing and maintaining student property.

Running a property business moves through phases:

- Sourcing and buying property

- Preparing and advertising the property for letting

- Managing the property

- Managing financial records

Most student landlords have two management options - the DIY approach or delegating to a letting agent.

Self-management problems

Dealing with one student let for a group of three or four sharing is easily manageable if the property is within easy distance of the landlord's home and you are prepared for some disruption to your life.

For some reason, a shared student let seems to generate hugely more maintenance and administration issues than letting the same property to a family. As a DIY landlord managing your own property, be prepared for all manner of call-outs, including:

- Phone calls and emails at all times to deal with 'problems' from replacing a light bulb to plumbing emergencies

- Chasing down tenants who have failed to pay their rent

- Ongoing maintenance, from clearing blocked drains to redecorating

- Cleaning common areas, like halls and stairs

- Gardening

- Marketing and screening prospective tenants

- Keeping the books and completing tax returns

The secret of managing multiple properties

It's not uncommon to come across student landlords who have five, 10, 20 or more letting properties. For them, investing in property is a full-time job and a lifestyle choice.

Managing five or more properties can lead to never-ending phone calls from 20 or more tenants, endless maintenance and piles of paper. Professional landlords find the key to running a profitable and efficient property business is systemising the process.

This means working to a schedule and compiling checklists and manuals detailing how to complete any job.

For help with systemising your property business - *see Appendix B: The Student Landlord Toolkit.*

Protecting Your Cash From Crooks

Before handing any cash over to a letting agent, play safe and find out how they safeguard cash for you and your tenants.

Unlike estate agents, letting agents are not regulated and cannot display the Office of Fair Trading (OFT) kite mark on their branding.

The industry operates several self-regulatory schemes - but the important point to look for is a client money protection scheme.

All letting agents belonging to these schemes run client accounts that hold rents separately from the firm's money:

■ Association of Residential Letting Agents (ARLA)

■ National Federation of Property Professionals (NFOPP)

■ The Law Society

■ The National Approved Letting Scheme (NALS)

■ The Royal Institution of Chartered Surveyors (RICS)

■ SafeAgent

ARLA is the leading industry self-regulatory scheme with tough membership rules that exclude one-man bands and uphold a bonding scheme to protect client cash in the event of financial problems.

The independent SafeAgent scheme is backed by many of the UK's largest letting agent chains - including Bushells; Winkworth; Belvoir Franchising; Northwood Franchising; Foxtons; Spicer Haart; Touchstone; Young London; and Linley & Simpson.

Knowing yourself

To decide if you want to manage your own property or hand the job to a letting agent, you need to appraise yourself honestly.

First, do you have the time to manage your letting business?

If you are coping with a full-time day job - especially if you work shifts or on a rota - adding another full-time responsibility may cause stress as all your time off will be spent dealing with your property business.

Next, do you have the knowledge or experience?

A landlord of a student letting property has some arduous legal responsibilities to consider, like fire prevention, health and safety and the general welfare of tenants and their visitors in a letting property.

Student lets may need planning permission, depending on where they are located, as well as licensing by the local council. A landlord also has a legal obligation to keep good financial records and to declare any profits to the tax man.

On top of this you also need some key personal attributes, like communication skills, patience and probably DIY experience.

Cutting corners to save money inevitably leads to larger, unforeseen problems further down the line. If you do not think you have what it takes to manage your student letting business, then consider a letting agent.

Benefits of hiring a letting agent

Handing the job of managing your student to a professional letting agent is an attractive proposition. A letting agent should have the qualification and experience to look after your property. You can opt for a fully-managed service or just a tenant-finding service.

Fully-managed service

For a fully-managed service, you pay the letting agent a percentage of the monthly rent to deal with any problems arising from the property and to act as a buffer between you and the tenants.

The service will cost anything up to 20% of the monthly rent plus VAT, but the hefty price should bring peace of mind and puts a buffer between you and your tenants, who should go to the letting agent with any problem or queries.

So what should you expect for your money? Management services will differ between letting agents, but the minimum should cover:

- Advertising and screening tenants, including referencing

- Pre-letting inspection and inventory

- Checking-in the tenants

- Handling customer service and emergency calls from tenants

- Arranging maintenance visits from reliable tradespeople

- Rent collection

- Regular property inspections

- Renewal reminders for HMO licences and safety certificates

Tenant-finding service

This is a much lower standard than a fully-managed service. For a fixed fee, a letting agent will normally advertise your property and screen tenants, including referencing and credit checks.

The rest is the responsibility of the landlord. The cost of this service varies greatly between agents, but expect to pay around £200 to let a property. The amount will adjust depending on the number of tenants in the property.

Landlord Insurance

Letting property is a business, and many business owners see the sense in insuring against risks that can damage cash flow and assets. A property business can take insurance against several risks. None are compulsory. These costs are paid by the business and tax reducers - *see Chapter 11 - All About Property Tax.*

Many landlord insurance policies come as bundled deals including buildings, contents and liability cover. This is a cheaper option providing you want the cover. More insurers offer portfolio insurance for landlords with several rental properties.

Good places to find competitive landlord insurance quotes are brokers and online comparison sites. Talking directly to an insurer will result in specific advice about their products and not necessarily the cheapest or best cover for you.

Make sure the insurance adviser is a 'whole of the market' firm rather than a tied adviser. That way you are more likely to find a competitive policy.

This section looks at the different types of insurance and the cover they offer:

Buildings insurance

Buildings insurance covers the repair costs of damage to the structure of the building. Examples are fire damage or replacing tiles after a storm.

Landlords with mortgaged properties will probably find a clause in the loan deed specifying the property should be insured at all times. If you have a leasehold property, buildings insurance is generally covered by the freeholder and paid for as part of the service charge.

Contents insurance

Tenants should take out separate, personal protection to cover their belongings. Landlords can also take out contents cover for furnished and unfurnished lets. These would cover carpets, curtains, white goods and garden tools.

Liability insurance

Liability cover protects landlords from lawsuits from tenants and visitors who are injured or suffer loss related to the property - an example would be a visitor slipping on stairs or a path and breaking a limb. This cover is relatively cheap and worth including with other policies.

Rent cover

Often called rent guarantee, this policy is expensive but guarantees rent if a tenant gets into arrears and refuses to leave. The risk depends on the type of tenants you target.

Singles in HMOs or housing benefit tenants are probably the most likely to run up arrears, but in truth, every tenant presents some sort of financial risk to a landlord.

This insurance may include cover for legal fees relating to an eviction.

Let-to-buy

Home insurance will not cover a let-to-buy property once the landlord moves out and a tenant is in place. Just about every home insurance policy has a clause that invalidates a claim if the owner takes in a lodger or tenant.

New landlords should tell their insurer if a tenant is moving in - make sure this is in writing and the insurer updates the policy accordingly.

Council Tax

Who pays council tax and when depends on the property and the tenants.

Landlords pay tax on empty properties, but have a six-month exemption if the property is unfurnished and possibly longer if the home is uninhabitable - for instance, has no kitchen or bathroom. This covers properties under refurbishment.

Full-time students do not pay council tax but have to apply to the council for an exemption. A university or college will provide proof of study. If the papers cover the summer holidays, the property will also be exempt while they are away.

Who pays the tax depends on the tenancy:

- Tenants, including students, pay council tax on homes let under a single tenancy and must make their own arrangements with the council for any exemptions

- Landlords pay council tax for HMOs and generally collect the money as an add-on to the rent

It's a good idea to drop the council a line as tenants move in or out of a property so they can issue the bills accordingly.

Finish And Furnishings

The starting point for a student let is figuring out what a student wants from their home and simply giving it to them.

If you are not sure what finish to aim for, check out accommodation websites that offer virtual tours. Failing that, go and view a property to get a feel for the market.

Landlords should remember the property is not their home, but a business. Prospective tenants want empty rooms with blank walls so they can add their finishing touches not yours, so keep decoration simple:

■ Painted walls are easy to keep looking good with a quick wipe over or brush up, but wallpaper is expensive, time-consuming to put up and difficult to keep in good repair

■ Put laminate or tiles on the floors in kitchens and bathrooms - they are quick and easy to clean and replace

■ Carpet is a good idea for halls, stairs and landings to keep the clatter of footsteps down

Students need a decent bed, comfortable seating, wardrobes and drawers for clothes, bookshelves and workstations for their laptops. Rooms also need plenty of sockets for powering phones, televisions, games consoles and other gadgets.

Good security is a must - both to exterior doors and windows and each room. Tenants should feel safe in their home and confident their possessions are secure.

Also, think about secure storage. Many students have cycles or motorbikes. Somewhere to keep suitcases, boxes and other not so regularly used belongings out of the living space is an attraction.

Landlord Obligations And Duties

Landlords have a legal duty to ensure the personal health and safety of anyone living at or visiting their property. Many of these obligations are laid down in various laws and upheld by decisions in court. Some are also included in standard assured shorthold tenancy agreements.

The basic guideline for a landlord is the property has to be maintained to the same standard as that on the first day of the tenancy. The tenant should also hand the property back to that standard, bearing in mind fair wear and tear. Sometimes landlords and tenants are involved in rows over their responsibilities. If in doubt, take legal advice, but below is an overview of the law.

Tenants' right of quiet enjoyment

Tenants have the right to live in their homes without unreasonable disturbance from the landlord or someone acting on the landlord's behalf. Common complaints include landlords entering rental properties with spare keys when the tenants are out.

Landlords can go inside a home in an emergency or to make repairs, but it's a good idea to arrange an appointment to carry out any work and to give at least 24 hours' notice, if not more.

Landlord's responsibilities for repairs

Repairs that the landlord should carry out include:

- Ensuring gas and electrical fittings meet safety standards

- Maintaining the structure of the building

- Looking after the internal fittings - like baths, showers, sinks and kitchen units

- Servicing and repairing heating and hot water systems

- Cleaning and looking after common areas shared by tenants - like halls, landings and stairs

Tenants' responsibilities for repairs

Tenants must not carry out any repairs or maintenance unless they are specifically included in a tenancy agreement.

A tenant should take care of a property and put right any damage that is not fair wear and tear. Fair wear and tear covers bumps, scrapes and scuffs that result from everyday living and replacing broken items, like crockery and glassware provided by a landlord.

Gas and electrical safety

Tenants should receive a copy of any current gas or electrical safety certificate when a tenancy agreement is signed. Gas installations and appliances must be checked by law at least once a year by a suitably qualified engineer.

Landlords have no legal obligation to check the electric installation in a buy-to-let, but they do have a duty of care to make sure any appliances and fittings are safe. A council can stipulate annual electric inspections as part of an HMO licence.

Energy Performance Certificates (EPCs)

Every letting property should have a valid EPC detailing the home's energy rating. An EPC is valid for 10 years or until a property is sold, when a new one is required. From June 2011, EPC rules changed and landlords must provide a certificate before marketing a property, not at some later date.

Furniture and furnishings safety

Fire safety regulations lay out minimum safety standards for letting a furnished property. All furniture should carry a fire safety label. The regulations apply to furniture and soft furnishings, including cushions, pillows and seat covers.

Linen, curtains and carpets are exempt. A landlord is not responsible for any furniture or furnishings taken into the property by a tenant.

Part 2
Dealing With Tenants

Chapter 5
Marketing A Student Let

● ●

- *Accreditation where it's due*
- *Setting the rent*
- *Finding the right tenants*
- *Countdown to viewing checklist*

● ●

Preparing a property for letting is only half the job. Think about your property business as a pregnancy. You have several months nurturing the bump and getting used to the idea. Some of that time is preparing for the birth, buying baby clothes and doing up the spare room as a nursery. Then comes the fateful day and everything changes.

All those issues you had as an expectant parent disappear and are replaced with a whole lot of new problems. Managing investment property is pretty much the same - six months or so of preparation to make your let ready for tenants without actually meeting one. Then you have to deal with tenants, collect rents and manage your property. This chapter delivers some important points about that all important job - marketing a student let.

Accreditation Where It's Due

Membership of accreditation schemes is voluntary, although attending a course run by a group may be part of house in multiple occupation (HMO) licensing conditions. Accreditation schemes aim to let landlords demonstrate that their properties comply with legal standards and that they operate good management practices.

The The AFS/Unipol code is the national accreditation scheme for student landlords.

Detailed information about accreditation is available from www.anuk.org.uk

How accreditation operates

Either a landlord or a property is accredited by a scheme. To gain accreditation, some landlords have to attend a course and pass a test or the property is rigorously inspected. The details of testing can vary between local councils.

Accreditation is retested at intervals and, if knowledge or standards slip, can be withdrawn.

Benefits of accreditation

ANUK hopes that landlords gain an edge over their competitors by attaining accreditation. Schemes may also offer other perks, like discounted insurance.

One of the main advantages is access to joint letting ventures with local councils and universities, who recommend tenants directly to accredited landlords.

Setting The Rent

Setting the rent is straightforward, but a lot of landlords bring in emotional factors that distort the calculation.

Just plucking a figure out of the air because it seems right won't do. You have to balance the property costs and tax against the market rate for student accommodation nearby.

Pegging the rent too high will mean tenants are difficult to find and you could carry the costs from other income, while floating the rent too low could mean your income does not fully cover your costs. Either is a financial disaster. Average rents for student lets in London and the regions are in *Table 2 Student property average rents and yields on page 13.*

Remember these figures are averages, and within the regions, rents will vary considerably between areas.

Check out the rents in your town by visiting www.accommodationforstudents. com which includes a comprehensive city by city, area by area guide to average rent. Be careful to pick comparable properties within half a mile or so for your rent analysis.

The idea is to look at properties students who view your properties are viewing nearby.

Factors that affect rents

Some corporate rental packages seem higher than those charged by private landlords. That's because they bundle their accommodation package into one monthly price to pay rather than adding charges.

Rent is important, but occupancy rate is more so. Occupancy is how much time tenants spend in your property as a percentage of the time it's available to rent.

Having a rental house with the tenants paying £5 less a week than you would like is better than having the house empty and paying the bills out of your own pocket.

Start by establishing your break-even point, which is the least amount of rent you must receive every month to pay the letting property bills. Next, look at comparable rental costs of similar properties around the neighbourhood where you are letting.

Now you can see the likely rent you will receive and the profits you will make.

Other local factors may affect the rent of your property. Points to think about are:

- Size of the accommodation

- Whether the rooms are en suite

- Are you bundling bills like utilities and broadband into the price?

- How close are you to campus?

- Are you offering onsite parking and storage?

- Do you offer additional services?

- What is the competition offering?

- Does the university offer halls accommodation?

It's important your property is neither too expensive nor too cheap for the area.

Agreeing the rent

Before any documents are signed, the landlord and tenant should agree how much rent is due, when the money should be paid and arrangements for periodic reviews.

If the rent is collected weekly, the landlord has a legal obligation to provide the tenant with a rent book. It's a good idea to give the tenant a dated receipt for any cash payments.

Keep a copy for yourself and ask the tenant to countersign to prove the amount and date paid.

Paying utility bills

Any good tenancy agreement will clarify who is responsible for paying utility bills.

Generally, the tenant is responsible for the bills, but often in a multiple let, the landlord pays and passes the cost on to the tenants as part of the rent. A good rule of thumb is whoever's name is on the account pays the bill.

Always check meter readings when moving a tenant in or out - and if you can, photograph the meter and ask the tenant to confirm the figures in writing. Landlords can call a utility company and let them know when tenants are moving.

If you employ a manager or letting agent, make sure who does this is agreed in your terms of business.

If utility bills are included in the rent, any tenancy agreement should include a clause on how this is adjusted if fuel costs rise. A clause letting the landlord increase the rent charge in line with the bills is generally acceptable, providing the tenant has reasonable warning of when and by how much the rent will rise.

Keep copies of the bills - they are needed for rental accounts and the tenant may ask to verify their fuel costs.

Bundling services into the rent

Some big corporate landlords bundle rent, utilities and other services into one monthly bill. This is often an attractive proposition for the tenant, because it's easier to budget for a single monthly payment - and the landlord does not have to continuously chase tenants to pay bills.

For a landlord, marketing is also simpler if broadband, wi-fi, and satellite or cable TV fully-loaded with sports, movies and music channels are included in the rent and utilities. For some rentals, extra services like cleaning and gardening can also be added to the mix.

Finding The Right Tenants

Generating interest in your rental property from the right sort of tenants is a trick of the trade. Unsuitable tenants are a waste of time and money - most landlords do not want to spend hours answering the phone and arranging viewings for tenants who will fail referencing or who will not sign on the dotted line.

Earlier in the chapter, one source of tenants was touched on - accreditation with your local college or university. The standards are high, but the returns are potentially good as you will receive a flow of inquiries from prospective tenants buoyed by the fact your property is 'approved'.

Accommodation for Students (www.accommodationforstudents.com) is the UK's leading student accommodation website. Landlords have been successfully finding good quality tenants since 2000, which is why it is so successful.

However if you don't want to put all your eggs in one marketing basket, here is a list of some other ways you can advertise for tenants.

Table: Advertising for Student Tenants

Method	Pros and cons	Hit rate
Flyers	Cheap and cheerful	Low
Newspapers	Unlikely to be seen outside the area	Low
Accreditation	Tried and trusted - gets straight to the source	High
Signage	OK for passers by	Low
Internet	Student housing portals are popular	High
Websites	Marketing your own website can be costly	Low
Noticeboards	Unlikely to be seen outside the area	Low
Property mags	Many cities have free property mags	High
Referral	Referrals can be the best recommendations	High
Letting agent	Only go with a specialist student firm	High

Some of these methods are time-consuming and costly while returning little or no results. First-year student tenants come from out-of-town, so they are unlikely to see local advertising - although many will sign up with a local letting agent.

Managing Property Viewings

If your property is popular with students and you have a flow of viewings, you need some way of keeping a note of who has called, what they have said and your impressions of them when you meet.

That way, after a flood of calls and appointments, you can sit down and consider each applicant on their own merits across a standard list of comparison points without having to rack your brains about who said what.

Having a crib sheet makes sure you have all the contact and financial information you need to help with weighing a decision.

The sheet comes in two parts - first an aide-memoire for answering the phone, and then another page for your impressions of the viewing.

Many landlords forget that taking calls and meeting viewers is a screening process for them - it's not just the tenant who is checking out you and your property.

It's just as important for the landlord to fidnd out about the tenants as well.

Playing Your Calling Cards Right

Some people like to leave a calling card, but in this case, you will make a record of everyone making an inquiry to rent a property. Have a list of simple questions ready - and follow the same template for every caller:

- ■ Name

- ■ Time and date of call

- Current address

- Contact number

- Email address

- Where did you hear about the property - for market research?

- Time and date of viewing

- Have you sent them directions?

- Do you have a car - for parking requirements?

- Do you have a rent guarantor?

- Your notes

Don't forget to take details of how the viewer found out about your property. This is valuable information that will help make your future marketing to more effective as you can narrow down the best places to advertise or which letting agents do a good job.

The rest of the sheet is for a viewing, and covers details like your impressions of the prospective tenants, financial arrangements and dates for moving in. Here are some suggestions for your viewing crib sheet:

- Viewing date and time

- Did they show up?

- Comments about the property

- Did they complete a rental application?

Countdown For Viewing Checklist

Preparing a property for letting means going through a checklist to make sure everything is in working order and no little tweaks or repairs are needed.

If you are new to buy-to-let, or unsure what is required by a tenant, here are some quick tips, but the list is not exhaustive:

- Clear any rubbish - this includes the garden, garage and any outbuildings, like sheds

- Check the plumbing - go round and turn all the taps and showers on, both hot and cold. Switch on the heating and bleed radiators

- Check any appliances - this includes stand-alone heaters, the cooker and fridge

- Check the lights - make sure all the bulbs work

- Check the electrics - make sure all plugs are safe and work

- Check locks and handles - this is important for security. Don't forget window locks and privacy catches on bathroom doors

- Check windows and curtains are clean. Any blinds should work

- Check bathrooms and kitchens are clean

- Check smoke and carbon monoxide detectors work

- Check the gardens are tidy, with beds and pots weeded and grass cut

- Check the carpets and floors are vacuumed/washed - start at the top and back of each floor and work towards the front door so you do not have to walk over cleaned areas

- Was a holding deposit paid?

- If so, how much?

- Your comments about the viewers

See Appendix B: Student Landlord Toolkit

Rooms With A View

If you have several viewers, you might want to arrange an 'open house' for a day.

Opening up for a few hours can save much time and stress involved with individual viewings. You will generate feedback about the property and inject a sense of urgency into a prospective tenant as they can see they have some competition.

You should be able to work the opening hours around events at the university, when students come up with their families for a look around. To make doubly sure anyone interested in renting your property has a chance of a viewing, try setting up arrangements at different times on different days.

All that hard work preparing the property to rent has been about bringing those viewers through the door.

Showing Off Your Property

If you have several viewers turning up at once, you are probably not going to give guided tours.

Have a property description sheet that gives the standard letting agent or estate agent information - room sizes, facilities in the house, distance from campus and the like. Make sure you get everyone's contact details as they arrive, because some viewers may turn up who you have not spoken to on the telephone. How you show off your property is down to you, but remember at some stage, most viewers like to be left alone so they can consider their new home at their own pace. If they come with friends or family, they may want to discuss the property in private.

Let them take their time, answer any questions and ask for comments. If they indicate they want to move in, ask each prospective tenant to complete a rental application form.

Why You Need A Rental Application Form

These forms are not just a waste of time, but are important for two reasons:

- You need standard comparison information to decide who is offered a tenancy

- You need to show that you are not discriminating against applicants by not taking their details for consideration

Do not take a joint application for a group of friends - you need a separate application from each person wanting to live at your property.

Have a separate form with each rental application that the viewer can sign to let you carry out a credit check. You should also verify identification with two documents - one with a photo ID, like a driving licence or passport, and the other proving their current address. Generally, this is a bank statement or other official document.

If the viewer is putting forward a guarantor for the rent, you also want them to complete a form and provide ID. A good idea here is not to accept someone living in rented accommodation as a guarantor - you really want someone who owns their own home. A homeowner has something to lose and a permanent address if the rent is not paid.

See Appendix B: Student Landlord Toolkit

Holding A Deposit

As a landlord, you want a financial commitment from someone who wants to rent your property. Most landlords have several rental applications, but not everyone is prepared to put their money up to confirm their intentions. Some tenants put in multiple applications in case they do not get offered the property they really want.

You are in business. It's not financial sense to take your property off the market for a tenant who does not commit to the deal. Not only that, but credit searches cost you time and money. A holding deposit is a non-refundable application fee that covers your costs. Check out your local letting agents, they will all charge a similar fee to cover administration costs.

Holding deposits are short-term solutions. The idea is to cover a landlord's costs for a couple of days - any longer and the prospective tenant should start paying daily rent.

Any serious tenant would have their deposit and first month's rent in place. They would only need a day or so to formalise the arrangements and transfer the money.

Don't get confused between a holding deposit and a tenancy deposit. They are not the same. A holding deposit is not money that needs covering under the tenancy deposit protection scheme.

See Page 80 Protecting Tenant Deposits for more about safeguarding deposits and Appendix B: Student Landlord Toolkit.

Chapter 6
Starting A Tenancy

- *How to screen your tenants*
- *Necessity is the mother of inventories*
- *Protecting deposits for tenants*
- *Consider a property guide*

Screening and choosing the right tenants becomes a lot easier when the process is sytemised to reduce the margin of error. The best student tenants are those who pay their rent on time and do not trash the place - other than that you can't hope for a whole lot more.

Once you are working to a system, it's pretty easy to weed out the time wasters and those you don't really like. In the previous chapter, the concept of inquiry and viewing cards was introduced as a template for gathering comparison information about your prospective tenants.

This chapter takes you to the next level - scoring your tenants to see who makes the grade and who to send packing.

It's the landlord version of the X-factor or Britain's Got Talent.

In effect, you are auditioning your prospective tenants to make reasoned business decisions. Over time, the process will become more intuitive and sophisticated, but to start, we need to set out a written profile of our perfect student tenant.

How To Screen Your Tenants

What do you want out of your student tenants? Probably no hassle and the rent paid on time - but you need to kiss a few frogs before you meet that ideal tenant.

Intoday's litigious society, a landlord must show that any tenancy decisions were made according to well-thought out and legal criteria.

If a letting agent manages the property or sources tenants, they should have a written selection policy.

Stamp out discrimination

The first point to remember about selecting a tenant is the Equality Act 2010. The law states that landlords cannot discriminate against anyone due to:

- Race

- Colour

- Gender

- Religion

- Marital status

- Disability

The Equality and Human Rights Commission has published a code of practice on racial equality in housing.

Landlords should observe this code because the recommendations are endorsed by Parliament and enforceable by the courts. Three codes are in force - one each for England, Scotland and Wales. Copies are available for download from the

Equality and Human Rights Commission website at http://www.equalityhuman-rights.com/

Taking references and guarantors

The problem with letting to students is they are too young to have a credit or rental history.

Without these, referencing is really not worth a lot. That's why most landlords ask for a rent guarantor - someone with the financial means to pay the bills if the tenant can't or won't.

The guarantor signs a legally-binding agreement which is enforceable in court, promising to pay the debts of the tenant.

Always seek a guarantor who is a homeowner - then they are traceable and have something to lose if the rent is not paid or the property is badly damaged.

Although references don't really come up to scratch for students, landlords should still verify identification and addresses for them - and the guarantors as well.

Scan photo ID - but if you do not have a scanner, take a picture of the document with your phone or a digital camera. Having a copy of ID puts paid to anyone claiming they are not the person that owes you money at a later date. Always credit check tenants and guarantors as well.

Landlords should also ask for a couple of names and landline telephone numbers for family who they can contact in case of an emergency. These details also give a landlord somewhere to start in tracking down a wayward tenant.

This section is a little cynical about how tenants may conduct themselves. Of course, the vast majority are decent, honest people who would not dream of failing to pay a bill, but the odd one or two cause the problems and it's better to be prepared.

Checking A Tenant's Credit History

Letting agents should check the credit history of a tenant as a matter of course. This is particularly important if a landlord has rent guarantee insurance on a property, as the insurer will void any claim if a credit check was not made before a tenant moved in.

Credit checks are not the holy grail of screening tenants, but they do help build a profile of them.

A credit search will reveal a tenant's financial history, like whether they have court judgments (CCJs), defaults or if they are bankrupt. The report will also show details of any loans and credit cards and whether payments are made on time.

What to look for on a credit search

Bad credit does not make a tenant a bad risk - many people have financial difficulties at some time due to unforeseen circumstances or bad luck, like redundancy or serious illness.

If someone has a whole lot of adverse information grouped around a date, it's probably because they had bad luck. Ask them why, and if the response is reasonable, there's no reason why you should not consider them as a tenant.

Alarm bells should start ringing if someone has regular, repeated bad credit information like defaults and missed payments. This is an indicator that they probably do not manage their money well and could end up skipping on rental payments.

Understanding Tenancy Agreements

Tenancy agreements are complicated legal documents that give landlords and tenants obligations and rights in relation to the renting of a property. Not all contracts are the same.

Tenants who take on an entire house or a self-contained flat in a block generally have an assured shorthold tenancy agreement, while someone taking a room in a shared house would have a licence to occupy.

Landlords should understand the difference as, under law, each agreement gives a tenant different rights to occupy a premises. This information is by no means exhaustive, and landlords are should consult a professional adviser before entering into any letting agreement.

Defining a tenancy

Three factors make someone's occupation of a property a tenancy rather than trespass:

- Exclusive possession of all or part of a property

- A fixed or periodic term to remain is possession

- Payment of rent

Once a tenancy is in place, the landlord should define whether the arrangement is an assured shorthold tenancy or a licence to occupy, because the rules governing each are different in law.

If a tenant does not have exclusive possession because they share, they are a licensee.

Calling a tenancy a licence won't wash with a court - it's not what a landlord calls the document but the rights that the agreement gives to the person staying at the property that count.

A fixed tenancy is an agreement to let a tenant move in with an agreement to vacate on a specific date, like a six-month assured shorthold tenancy agreement. A periodic tenancy is one with out a fixed end date.

What is an assured shorthold tenancy?

An assured shorthold tenancy (AST) is sometimes called a 'default' letting agreement, because if a landlord has no written contract, the arrangements between the landlord and tenant revert to an AST.

The term refers to the tenancy agreement and covers the legal rights and obligations of the landlord and the tenant.

The agreement can last for any term, but most are for six months and few landlords agree to more than 12 months.

A tenancy agreement creates a legal interest in the property that restricts the landlord's right to take possession.

On the other hand, the benefit for landlords is no reason is needed to take possession of a property once the correct notice is served to end the AST.

If a landlord wants a tenant to leave, the notice is generally two months, while if the tenant wishes to go, they have to give one month's notice. A landlord has to request the tenant to quit by completing and serving a Section 21 notice. The section refers to the relevant clause in the Housing Act 1988.

If the tenant fails to leave, the landlord can pursue eviction through a county court.

What is a licence to occupy?

A tenant has a much reduced right to stay in a property under a licence to occupy in comparison to an assured tenancy agreement. A licence to occupy differs from a tenancy agreement because the arrangement does not create an interest in the property.

Guests at hotels and bed-and-breakfasts or lodgers have a licence to occupy. The key difference between a tenancy and a licence is exclusive possession. Most students living in a shared house would have a licence rather than a tenancy.

Say what you mean - in writing

Landlords are not obliged to have written tenancy agreements for tenancies of three years or less.

However friendly the landlord and tenant may be, relationships sour and proving who said what in court is a lottery for a landlord trying to take possession of a property.

Written tenancy agreements should clearly lay out the duties and responsibilities of both sides. Evicting a tenant who does not have a written tenancy agreement is a can of worms and probably means a court is like to revert to a standard assured tenancy agreement as the basis of any judgement anyway.

Always have a tenant sign the agreement before moving in. After moving in, a tenant does not have to sign an agreement and the absence of any agreement makes eviction procedures a lot more complicated.

Landlords cannot let tenants live in a property on probation without a tenancy agreement that might come along later if the arrangement works out for both parties.

Watch out for unfair terms

The Unfair Terms in Consumer Contracts Regulations 1999 apply to tenancy agreements as well as other consumer contracts.

The rules do not affect the basic terms of a tenancy, like setting the rent, but do protect the rights of the tenant.

The rules do not stop landlords including specific terms in an agreement - it's the way they are written that count. A good example concerns pets - some landlords have a blanket ban on pets because they can destroy fixtures and fittings or place undue wear on tear on carpets and decorations.

Saying 'no pets allowed' in the tenancy agreement could be construed unfair, while a clause stating 'pets are allowed with the express written permission of the landlord, which will not unreasonably be withheld' is better.

Then, if the tenant wants to keep a huge dog in a property, permission can be reasonably withheld on the basis the animal would inconvenience other tenants, is too large for the house and so on.

For more information, go to the Office of Fair Trading website at http://www.oft. gov.uk/shared_oft/reports/unfair_contract_terms/oft356.pdf

Necessity Is The Mother of Inventories

Arguments over whether the landlord or tenant should pay for damage to a property at the end of a tenancy is a big cause of friction.

These disagreements are the source of a huge number of complaints to the official bodies that manage tenancy deposit protection schemes. The bodies have a mediation scheme to help resolve the rows, and have jointly published a guide, 'Your Guide to deposits, disputes and damages' .

The guide outlines the methodology behind arbitrating disputes, and recommends that landlords and tenants should compile an inventory of a rental property at the outset and end of a tenancy.

Download a free copy from this link: http://www.mydeposits.co.uk/sites/default/files/mydep%20DDD%20ADR.PDF

Landlords and letting agents should also make sure regular property inspections are carried out during the tenancy.

10 Tips For A Perfect Inventory

■ Be systematic - start at the front gate and tour the property room by room

■ List every item down to the last teaspoon, otherwise there's not much point if the inventory is incomplete.

■ Photograph or video all the items listed - some inventories have hundreds of images attached on a disk. Digitally date the images or print copies and ask the tenant to date and sign them

■ Always conduct the inventory with the tenant present

■ Ask the tenant to comment on the condition of every item and to countersign the inventory form

■ Give a copy of the inventory to the tenant

■ If you both agree that an item has a scuff or mark, photograph the mark and put a ruler alongside so a third party can get some idea of the size. Think like TV's CSI and those L-shaped rulers - you can stick them to a door or wall with blu-tac

■ Don't forget garages, gardens and sheds - and check the loft

■ If any action or repairs are needed as the result of the inventory, keep a record of exactly what was agreed and when the action was taken to remedy the problem

■ Have a key to describe the terms used to score the condition of items and avoid terms like 'fair' or 'OK' that are ambiguous. Attach the key to the inventory and consistently use the terms throughout the document

For instance, if a new carpet is listed, the condition is 'unmarked'

This is an aspect of their job that many letting agents fail to complete - they are consistently fobbed off when trying to make appointments with tenants to make the inspections or do not adequately record issues. Good inventories and subsequent follow-up inspections are crucial for landlords.

In one extreme case, a tenant built a two-storey brick extension on the rear of a letting property that was not spotted by the letting agent. Landlords are consistently awarded compensation and costs from the deposit when producing an effective inventory signed and agreed by the tenant as evidence - especially if they include photographic or video evidence.

What is an inventory?

An inventory is a detailed list of the items in a home and condition of the property taken at the time a tenant moves in, at any regular property inspection and again when at check out when a tenancy agreement ends. Landlords and letting agents often undertake the task themselves, but should make sure any document and attached images is of good evidential value, while agreed and countersigned by the tenant.

Hiring an inventory clerk

Inventory clerks are professionals who prepare watertight inventories for landlords and letting agents. They are regarded as impartial expert witnesses by courts and arbitrators. Inventory clerks can be found via the website of the Association of Independent Inventory Clerks at *www.aiic.uk.com*

Protecting Deposits For Tenants

Tenancy deposit protection (TDP) schemes make sure landlords and letting agents keep safe any money handed over as a bond or deposit. All assured short-hold tenancy agreement deposits in England and Wales must be protected by law, while a similar scheme is about to start in Scotland.

How tenant deposit protection works

In law, a deposit or bond remains the property of the tenant even if handed over to a landlord or letting agent to meet the terms of a tenancy agreement.

A TDP scheme guarantees the deposit is handed back to a renter when they leave the home, provided they have kept to the terms of any tenancy agreement and caused no damage to the property. If the landlord does not place the deposit on protection, the tenant may claim a penalty in court. The landlord will also lose some rights to take possession of the rented property.

Landlords must provide the following information in writing to the tenant within 30 days of receiving the deposit:

- Details of the TDP holding the deposit

- Information about the scheme's dispute resolution service

- Instructions on releasing the deposit

- Returning a deposit when the tenant or landlord is absent

- How the TDP scheme protects the deposit

- Confirmation of the deposit paid and the rented property's address

- Contact details for the landlord and/or letting agent

- Contact details of any third party paying the deposit

- Services covered by the deposit

- Reasons why a landlord can retain all or part of the deposit

- How the tenant can dispute the amount retained from a deposit

Who keeps the deposit?

The government has approved three independent TDP schemes that hold the money for the duration of the tenancy.

Returning a deposit to a tenant

At the end of the agreement, the money is reclaimed and, under certain circumstances, the landlord can keep all or some of the cash to cover the cost of repairing any missing or damaged items.

If the tenant and landlord dispute the claim for loss or damage, each TDP scheme has an adjudicator who will look at the evidence from both sides and recommend a solution.

Consider A Property Guide

Experienced landlords will know the questions tenants ask time after time - they also want tenants to take responsibility for the property.

Putting together a frequently-asked-questions guide to a property is an excellent idea. Giving the tenant a folder with essential information is good customer service, but also stops phone calls about basics like how to operate the timer on the cooker or settings on the washing machine.

For students new to the area, some information about local doctors, dentists and where to dump rubbish goes a long way to proving to the council that you are a responsible landlord if neighbours complain about your tenants or student tenants in the area in general.

List whatever information is relevant to your property:

■ Locations of stopcocks and fuses

■ Boiler instructions - like setting the timer, running hot water only and relighting if it goes out

■ Light bulbs - the wattage and type, ie bayonet or screw fit

■ Instruction books for the cooker, washing machine and fridge etc

■ How to clean floors and carpets - detergents to use and dealing with spills

■ Rubbish collection day and where the council collect from

■ Contact details for the landlord and/or letting agent

Include lots of images to show buttons to press, switches to flick and levers to turn etc. The more detailed and basic the guide, the less likely the tenant is to call.

Dealing with damp

Damp from condensation is one of the biggest problems for landlords in rental houses.

The common scenario is no damp is listed on the inventory, but at check-out, rooms have black mould on the walls. The usual cause is a lack of ventilation when cooking, taking a shower or drying washing inside the property.

Include a 'help sheet' in the property guide that explains how this problem occurs and how to keep the property properly ventilated. It's a good idea to comment that costs of putting the damp problem right will be incurred by the tenant if they have not followed the instructions.

Blocked sinks and drains

This is another common scenario - the drains worked perfectly well at check-in but are blocked at the end of the tenancy. Include a list of what can go down the drain and what can't in your property guide.

Many landlords then point out to the tenant that if a drain cleaner has to be called out and the problem arises from something they have done, they will have to pay the bill.

Chapter 7
During A Tenancy

- *Keeping those rents rolling in*
- *Dealing with repairs and complaints*
- *Visiting a rented out property*
- *Handling problem tenants*

A landlord's work is never done and certainly does not stop when the tenants move in - and like most things, tasks expand to fill the time available. Unless you have an effective tenant management system, you will find yourself rushing around dealing with complaints, sorting out repairs and chasing rents.

Professional landlords have a policy for dealing with these issues. Take it as read that sooner or later a tenant will not pay the rent, appliances will break down, drains will block and pipes will leak.

Rather than act like an emergency service fighting fires and rushing to the next potential disaster, put that policy in place and tell the tenants what to expect in advance.

Most landlords will say that buying and readying a property for letting presents one catalogue of problems, while dealing with the tenants brings another set.

Some joke their letting business runs really smoothly until the paying customers are involved.

Joking aside, the most important consideration once tenants have moved in is cash flow. Good landlords respect the old adage that 'cash is king' and realise that without rents hitting the bank, they have no business.

Keeping Those Rents Rolling In

Most students are reliable with money and even those who struggle to pay the rent on time don't start out with any intention of building arrears. Remember, most are living away from their parents for the first time and probably haven't had to budget and pay bills before.

For landlords, collecting rent is likely to become harder as part-time jobs dry up giving students that extra cash, and tuition fees rise.

That's why a guarantor with property who has something to lose is so important - *see Page 73 - Taking references and guarantors.*

You can decrease the chances of tenants sliding into arrears by setting out a rent policy and by firmly enforcing the rules.

Reminding the tenants of the obligation to pay

Start as you mean to go on with your tenants and remind them from the start that part of the deal for them living in your house is that they pay the rent in full and on time.

When the tenancy agreement is signed, have an extra sheet about the rent - how much, when payment is due and what happens if payment is missed. Give them a copy of the document with the tenancy agreement.

Rent collection dos and don'ts

You are the landlord and how you run your business is up to you - but managing the rent is a key a task that defines the success of your rental business. No rent coming in equals finding money from somewhere else to pay the bills - no rent means a landlord must find more cash to subsidise running costs.

Clearly, a business cannot afford to run this way. Effectively, the tenants are benefitting from an unauthorised overdraft from the landlord by paying the rent late.

Here are some tips for dealing with rents:

■ **Match rent days with pay days**

> Most students receive their loans and grants in three instalments during the academic year - the dates will vary but generally they are the start of the year at the end of September, January and April

■ **Let tenants pay by standing order**

> Setting up a standing order means tenants do not have to remember to make the payment

■ **Keep calm if the rent is late**

> Your tenant may have a good reason for paying late, so going in heavy-handed with threatening letters can make the relationship antagonistic, nevertheless, late rent is serious and needs action

■ **Make personal contact**

> Do not harass your tenants, but make sure they understand you will call and ask for an explanation for late rent. They are less likely to avoid paying if they know you will pay a visit

■ **Charging late payment fees**

> Penalty payments can provoke controversy. On the pro side, why

shouldn't the tenant bear the cost of their actions, while setting a fee too high is unenforceable in court.

■ **Accepting part payments**

If a tenant cannot pay in full, accepting a part payment is not a good idea because accepting the cash negates any notices already served and you will have to restart legal proceedings.

Evicting a tenant

This book is not a legal guide - the tenant eviction process is outside the scope of the advice and a last resort.

Evicting a tenant is a serious legal step and landlords should take independent legal advice before starting the process.

Dealing With Repairs And Complaints

Even brand new homes need snagging, and the extra wear-and-tear of a group of students will result in queries, complaints and repairs.

Student tenancies are often two or three-year customer cycles. The cost of finding new tenants eats into rental profits, so it makes sense to offer good customer service to try and keep them happy - and to encourage them to book again for the next academic year.

With this in mind, any professional student landlord will tell you not to give out your mobile number or your phone will ring day and night with sometimes the most mundane calls.

Think about what you would want from a landlord if you were a student tenant - and then give that back as your service.

Taking calls from tenants

Offering excellent customer service is one way to keep problems to a minimum. If you have a problem with something you paid for, you want a quick and efficient resolution. Your tenants are the same about their homes. Too many landlords view complaints as chores instead of an important part of their business.

The tenant will want to call as soon as something goes wrong. If a landlord has several tenants in more than one property, that can mean a seemingly never-ending chain of calls at all hours.

Clearly, just as the tenant has a right to privacy, so does a landlord. Strike a balance that satisfies the tenants and your needs as well.

Set up a complaints hotline

Give your tenants an email address and telephone number for dealing with non-emergency maintenance and tenancy issues. Commit to responding to the messages but make clear you will only do this in normal business hours.

Defuse the stress with updates

Most property problems sort themselves out quite easily, but the worst way to handle them is not to tell the tenant what is going on - keep them informed of progress. If workmen cancel appointments or spare parts are difficult to find, explain the situation to defuse stress.

Sending in workmen

One of a tenant's basic rights is privacy. That means a landlord or workmen cannot turn up at any time and expect the tenant to let them in. If possible, let the tenant and workman make the appointments between themselves to save you shuttling between the two.

If they cannot agree a time and the defect could cause more damage to the property, then a landlord has a right to act - the tenancy agreement should provide the key to what to do in these circumstances.

Visiting A Rented Property

From time to time, the landlord or letting agent should regularly visit a letting property - about once every six months is a reasonable interval.

This does not include maintenance visits if tenants report a problem.

The visit is to check the property for any work that might need carrying out and to make sure the terms of the tenancy agreement are met.

Many landlords find a checklist helps by prompting what to look for. Previous checklists can also help as a reminder about problems spotted on previous visits and what action was taken to resolve the issues.

Unless a tenant agrees, a landlord must give at least 24 hours notice of a visit - and explain why the call is necessary. Different rules apply to buy-to-lets and shared houses - houses in multiple occupation or HMOs.

A landlord can only enter a buy-to-let rented under an assured tenancy agreement by appointment with the tenants, even if the property is let to several individuals on a joint tenancy.

However, the landlord is free to enter the communal areas of a shared house let as rooms on a licence at any reasonable time.

Looking Out For Human Rights

Many landlords might well ask what human rights have to do with letting rental property, but a landmark European Court of Human Justice case concerning a family that rented a home in Sweden has added to the regulatory burden.

The brief details of the case was the family wanted satellite TV, but their landlord would not agree to them erecting a dish on the outside of the building.

The family claimed this infringed their human rights - namely a freedom to access information without interference.

The European Court agreed and ruled that the landlord was wrong not to let the family put up a satellite dish - and ordered him to pay compensation of £12,000.

The ruling is important, not because providing tenants with satellite TV is a human right, which it is not, but because a burden is placed on landlords to let tenants have broadband, cable and satellite TV installations at the property.

Problem Tenants

The majority of tenancies come and go without any problems, but sooner or later a difficult tenant will come along.

Not paying the rent was dealt with earlier in this chapter, but rent arrears is not the only difficulty that can arise.

Some tenants have no respect for their neighbours or their homes. They damage property, make too much noise, keep late hours and do not clear up rubbish. Other problems can involve subletting and sneaking in pets.

Take reasonable action

Not every infraction by a tenant should trigger a red alert and eviction. Just like the government's defence security alerts, a landlord's reaction should gently glide through various levels of response.

The first port of call is always the tenancy agreement. A well-written agreement should clearly lay out the standards of behaviour landlords and tenants should expect from each other.

Document complaints and responses

Keep a tenant diary detailing any complaints from neighbours, the council or police and the action taken. Discuss the problem with your tenant and consider issuing them with a tenancy violation letter. Keep a record of minor complaints, because these can add up over a period of time.

A template letter is included in Appendix B: Student Landlord Toolkit.

Unlawful Evictions

Even the most annoying tenants have rights in law, and landlords cannot evict someone without carefully following the laid down legal process.

This guide is not a guide to eviction. If you have problems with a tenant, take independent legal advice from the outset. Do not take free opinions from councils or homeless organisations because, often, these will look at the problem from the view of the tenant.

Getting eviction wrong is costly - paying a few pounds for good advice should pay off in the long-run.

Chapter 8
Ending A Tenancy

- *Getting ready for move-out day*
- *What is normal wear and tear?*
- *Special move-out circumstances*
- *Watch out for the insurance trap*

Tenants moving on is a fact of rental business life. Sometimes it's a shame to say goodbye, and in other cases departure cannot come quick enough. Like any other part of letting, a good landlord should not leave the process to chance, but should have a well-oiled strategy in place to ease the fateful day for everyone.

A slick move-out procedure is good for both sides. Landlords need to think about a whole number of legal and marketing actions that are triggered as a result of the tenant giving written notice to quit the property.

In one way, moving out starts when a tenants moves in, as the tenancy agreement and covering letter should include details of giving notice to quit.

The inventory also lays a foundation for the expected condition of the property when the tenant leaves. Landlords who are taking action to possess a property need to refer to the tenancy agreement to make sure any termination or eviction remains inside the law. If not, expect to pay expensive compensation and expensive legal costs for illegal eviction or harassment.

Getting Ready For Move-out Day

Tenants are notoriously unreliable at following the legal conditions laid out in a tenancy agreement, but expect a landlord to strictly follow their obligations to the letter.

Rather than give specific information about moving out, a landlord is more likely to receive a quick phone call or a passing comment in a conversation with the tenant.

To make sure both sides completely understand their rights and obligations, include a notice to vacate as part of any welcome pack.

This template letter should cover all the relevant information and specific dates, avoiding misunderstandings. When a tenant sends over a written notice to quit, the response should be a moving out information letter.

This letter should tell tenants how to ready the property for a final inspection and arrangements for returning the deposit.

See Appendix B: Student Landlord Toolkit for template letters

Checking The Property

The final inspection is the major event of moving out. Schedule the check with a time that the tenants have moved out their furniture and belongings for two reasons - first, to make sure nothing is left behind and second, to make sure no defects are hidden.

In reality, few tenants hang around for the final inspection and even less bother to come back once they have moved on.

Go through the property with the inventory the tenant approved and signed as correct and note any issues or defects.

Don't forget normal wear and tear is not a defect or damage that the tenant should pay for.

What is 'normal' wear and tear?

The majority of complaints handled by the Property Ombudsman relate to tenants disagreeing over whether all or part of a deposit was kept fairly by the landlord.

Landlords can retain money from the deposit to pay for replacing or repairing damage items. The issue is what is 'normal' wear and tear?

Wear and tear is damage or deterioration arising from normal use of a property. Landlords should expect scuffs and scrapes, but not burns in the carpet or holes in the walls. The term is not explained in law and is very much a case considering the merits of each incident.

Who pays for putting damage right?

A landlord has a lawful right to make certain deductions from the tenant's deposit:

- Unpaid rent

- Damage beyond normal wear and tear

- Replacing lost keys

- Cleaning

Give the tenant a comprehensive report detailing the scope of the repairs. That means explaining the nature of the defect, where it is and the cost of the repair.

If the cost of putting the defect right fits into the schedule of allowed deductions, then give the tenant the repair report and keep the cash. Returning a deposit has no time limit, but good practice would suggest dealing with repairs and handing the money back should take less than 30 days.

Returning the deposit

In most cases, the tenant will be eager for the return of any money, as the cash is probably needed as a deposit on another rental property. Send the tenant an account for the deposit with a cheque. The account should state the amount of the deposit, listing any deductions and comments.

Some tenants will call to pick up the money, while others may not leave an address on the notice to quit form. If you have no forwarding address, send the account and cheque to the tenant at the rental property just vacated - sometimes the tenant has arranged to have the mail forwarded.

If not, the cheque will come back to you. Keep the postmarked letter to prove you have tried to send the deposit on in case the tenant complains to the Property Ombudsman.

See Appendix B: Student Landlord Toolkit for template letters

Special Move-out Circumstances

Not all tenancies run a full term before the tenant moves out. All sorts of problems and complications can arise that mean tenants change their plans. Here are some quick tips on dealing with some of the most common occurrences:

■ Housemates part company

Sharers may move into together as a couple or as joint tenants and then, for some reason, one moves out. Often, the tenant who is leaving wants some of the deposit back. Tell the tenants it's not your problem and let them sort out any refund among themselves.

■ **Repairs cost more than the deposit**

Sometimes rent arrears, repairs and cleaning come to more than the amount of the deposit. A good tip is to account for the deposit that you hold to cover damage first and then rent arrears. The reason is damage is harder to prove in court than arrears. Take a view on pursuing the cash in court - the time and money this costs may not be worth proving you are right in the long-term.

■ **Property left behind**

If a tenant leaves property behind when moving out, special legal rules apply. Write to the tenant asking them to collect their property, then shift the items into storage so the home can be rented out again. After three months, sell the property and deduct your costs - the balance belongs to the tenant and they have six years to claim the cash.

Viewings Before A Tenant Moves Out

This can be a tough one for landlords. Landlords obviously want the shortest possible void - the time between tenancies - but despite the stress of letting a property out in double quick time, arranging viewings while the departing tenant is still in situ is difficult.

Certainly if the tenant is leaving under a cloud, you do not want to have them offer opinions about you, or your property, to potential new tenants. The same legal rules apply to viewings as any other property visit, so tenants should have at least 24 hours' notice of an appointment. In reality, unless the tenants is willing, line viewings up for after they have moved on.

Watch Out For The Insurance Trap

Obviously landlords want insurance cover for properties between tenancies, but watch out for the unoccupied property trap that can void a claim.

To many insurance firms, an unoccupied home is where no one has lived in the property for 30 consecutive days. Check landlord buildings and contents insurance to make sure that cover is maintained while a property is empty.

Some insurers expect property owners to drain down water systems if the property is empty during the winter to avoid pay outs for burst pipes.

See page 51 for more about landlord insurance.

Part 3
Looking After
The Finances

Chapter 9
All About Property Tax

● ●

- *Understanding property tax*
- *Tax and a typical landlord*
- *Telling the tax man about income tax*
- *Keeping a property register*

● ●

Tax cheats never prosper and HM Revenue and Customs is applying increasingly aggressive tactics to chase down those who are evading paying their dues. Landlords are one of the key targets in this campaign to raise more money for the Treasury coffers.

Tax offices have finally embraced technology to track down property investors who do not pay tax.

HMRC is now interlinked with other government agencies and council departments for the first time to give a broader picture of who owns property and who lives there.

The crucial link in the chain is the Land Registry. HMRC can now access all Land Registry records, which on their own reveal very little. When they are cross-referenced against the electoral roll, council tax data and housing benefit payment records, the picture is different.

From these records, the tax man can tell who owned a property, for how long and whether the home was let to tenants. This indicates whether the owner should have declared rental income or if capital gains tax was due on the sale of a property.

Coupled with new rules that let tax inspectors check how well 50,000 small business keep their financial records every year and revised fines for failing to file tax returns and pay the amounts due, the outlook for landlords who do not toe the tax line looks bleak.

Understanding Property Tax

Property tax does not really exist - it's a mix of several taxes that interact with each other. The main taxes for property investors are income tax and capital gains tax:

- **Income tax** is paid on rental profits of a buy-to-let business, regardless of the location of the property. So if you are a UK taxpayer and let property in Europe or the USA, you pay income tax on your profits.

  Of course, you may also pay the tax authorities in the country where the property is located. You do not pay twice on the same profits because most countries have double taxation treaties to remove the risk.

- **Capital gains tax (CGT)** is paid on the 'chargeable gain' an investor earned on the value of a property during the time they owned the asset. The property can be located in the UK or overseas, and just as with income tax, the double taxation risk is removed.

Other taxes may come into play, like stamp duty, but income tax and CGT are the big two.

Who Pays Property Tax?

The rule of thumb is tax follows ownership of a property, and an owner is someone who benefits financially from letting or selling a property.

Tax And A Typical Landlord

A typical landlord started trading with one or two buy-to-lets making a rental loss because of the cash spent on refurbishments and high mortgage interest rates.

Because no profits were made and no tax was due, many landlords just did not bother to submit a tax return.

Over the next year or two, they bought two or three more letting properties and suddenly, the paperwork becomes a lot more time-consuming and complicated.

The landlord believes because the tax man has not caught up that the problem has gone away.

The problem is HMRC can back-track any number of years once a tax inquiry is opened. As a number of years have passed, those rental losses that were cancelling out taxable profits have dropped away and low mortgage rates mean the level of expenses claimed against profits has decreased as well.

The likely result is a compliance letter. The letter from the tax man will politely suggest a landlord may have had income from property that remains undeclared and suggests preparing rental accounts for the years in question.

The letter is the start of a tax investigation. HMRC already knows the landlord had property income, now they want to know how much is owed.

Some landlord tax inquiries have stretched back to the late 1990s, with the stress and cost of preparing tax accounts from missing records and relating to properties that were sold some years ago.

Interest on unpaid tax accrues at a daily rate, while fines and surcharges can run into thousands on tax bills dating back several years.

That can be someone who picks up a share of the rent or a slice of the proceeds from a sale.

Ownership is often obvious from Land Registry records, but not all owners appear on the deeds. The tax man will want to know who owns a property to nail who should pay tax.

Remember tax is not an opt-in - the obligation is on the person earning income from property to report to the tax man, not to wait until asked.

Similarly, a husband and wife team cannot decide to give rental profits to the wife because the husband is a higher rate taxpayer without officially transferring his share.

Tax returns have to tie up with shares of ownership - so if a husband and wife own a property 50:50, then half the rental profits go to each unless specific arrangements have been made to the contrary.

When Is Property Tax Paid?

Just as the rules lay out who pays income tax on property profits, another set of rules defines when the tax is paid.

The date of first letting is the key. This is the day the first tenant in the first rental property pays rent - generally, the day the first tenancy agreement or licence started.

When the property was bought or when the tenant moved in are not relevant - before the date of first letting a landlord did not have a property business because no rent was due, therefore no commercial transaction took place.

The first rental accounts run from the date of first letting until the following April 5. Subsequent tax years run from April 6 to the following April 5 until the end of the business.

The tax returns for reporting this income have three filing dates:

- October 31 following the tax year end for filing a paper tax return

- December 30 following the tax year end if a landlord has a salary and wants his or her tax code adjusted to collect the tax

- January 31 following the tax year end for filing a tax return online

If any income tax is due that is not collected from a tax code adjustment, then the payment must be made by January 31 following the tax year end.

Assuming a landlord's first tenancy agreement runs from October 1, 2013, then the filing and tax dates are:

- Tax year - runs from October 1, 2013 until April 5, 2014

- Filing date - January 31, 2015, although special circumstances could mean filing earlier or later

- Income tax payment date: January 31, 2015

Telling The Tax Man About Income Tax

Letting the tax man know a property business has started trading is the responsibility of the taxpayer. The crucial point is not whether the business makes a profit, but that the taxpayer has an additional stream of income.

Landlords must tell their tax office they have rental income straight away - or by October 5 following the end of the tax year when the income was first received.

For example, the date of first letting is January 1, 2011. The tax year ends on April 5, 2011, so October 5, 2011 is the latest date for reporting the extra income.

Deciding to file a tax return

HM Revenue and Customs decides who files a tax return, not an individual tax-payer. The taxpayer must tell HMRC about rental income so a tax inspector can decide whether to call for the filing of a return.

HMRC may decide not to send a notice requesting a return, but if they do send one, even if no tax is due, the taxpayer must file a return.

Telling The Tax Man About Capital Gains

So far the discussion has covered income tax on rental profits. The second important property tax is capital gains tax (CGT).

The CGT trigger is disposal of part or all of a property. Disposal means selling, gifting or transferring a share or part share of a rental property to a third party.

The good news is switching property shares between spouses or civil partners is exempt from CGT - but most other transfers involve tax, even though a number of reliefs that reduce the amount to pay are available.

If you dispose of property to someone other than a spouse or civil partner, nothing needs to be reported to the tax man. Tell HM Revenue and Customs about any other disposal by October 5 after the end of the tax year when the transaction took place.

For example, a letting property was sold in September 2012. The tax year ends on April 5, 2013 and notification to HMRC is due by October 5, 2013.

Accounting For Pre-Letting Expenses

The technical term here is 'pre-letting expenses', which are the costs a property investor has to cover before the date of first letting.

Dealing with these expenses is simple - first separate them out as capital costs or day-to-day business payments. Capital costs go to the property register - the details are in the next section.

The day-to-day costs are entered in the rental accounts as if they were incurred on the first day of letting - providing:

■ Any services, like labour charged by a workman was incurred up to six months before the date of first letting

■ Any goods were charged up to three years before the date of first letting

Keeping A Property Register

It's easy to lose track of paperwork, dates and other tax information if you own several letting properties over a number of years.

A property register is a good way to keep track of the important details for each property and owner. The register is simply a log book for each property for recording capital expenses and changes of ownership.

A property register is the primary tax document that shows who is entitled to rental profits and the proceeds of any sale.

How property usage affects tax

The property register keeps a record of how the property was used - different usages dictate whether any tax was due; if so, what type of tax and who pays.

During ownership, a property can switch between uses several times. The property uses that affect landlords renting out homes are:

■ **Buy-to-let or house in multiple occupation (HMO)** - the rental business models may vary, but for tax purposes this type of rental is the same. Owners pay income tax on rental profits and capital gains tax on any chargeable gains on disposal of all or part of their share of ownership.

■ **Living in the property as a main home** - the property is exempt from capital gains tax during this time

■ **Holiday letting** - renting to tourists on short-term lets. Income tax is paid on rental profits and CGT on disposal

■ **Uncommercial letting** - this covers letting a friend or relative stay in a property for free or a discounted rent. Uncommercial lets are excluded from rental property accounts, so no tax is due on any rent received below a commercial rate, but no expenses for repairs or other business expenses are available. CGT is due on disposal

What to list in a property register

The property register starts on the first day of ownership and runs until a property is sold or otherwise disposed of.

Here are some of the most common entries:

■ Date of purchase

■ How much was paid for the property or the open market value on taking over ownership

■ Incidental buying costs - these include stamp duty and legal costs

■ Improvement costs - these are expenses that add to the property, like a loft extension, conservatory or garage

Repairs are not counted - they go in the rental accounts

■ Spending on protecting the title - like legal costs to establish a fence line

■ Incidental sale costs - estate agents charges and legal fees

■ Date of disposal

■ Disposal price

Other important information includes:

■ Property use - dates when the property was let to buy-to-let tenants, rented out as a holiday let, an uncommercial let or when one of the owners lived there as their main home

■ Date of first letting

■ Tenancy agreements

■ Owners - including the date they became an owner, the percentage share of ownership and relationship with other owners ie spouse or civil partner. Other ownership information is the open market value of the property on assuming ownership and disposal, whether they owned and lived in the property as a main home, and if so, the dates

Documents to keep with the property register

Keep the documents that prove the information in the register - like solicitor's letters, bills from tradespeople and any written valuations.

Tagging Financial Records

Tagging financial records is all about setting cost centres. A landlord's cost centres fall into three categories - each rental property, capital costs and general business expenses.

Tagging income and expenses by property lets each owner extract the figures they need for their tax returns:

- Capital costs go to the property register

- Income from tenants, day-to-day running costs and general business expenses go to the rental accounts

This tagging also lets property investors drill down to see exactly how much each property earns or loses - and allows analysis for yield to show the return on investment as well.

The other advantage is tagging means each owner can extract the appropriate figures from the rental accounts for their tax returns.

This is worked out from the property register that keeps a record of shares of ownership.

For example, if a property makes a profit of £3,000 and three owners are shown on the property register with owner 1 holding a 50% share and the others each with a 25% share, then the profits are allocated as £1,500 to owner 1 and £750 each to the remaining owners.

Tag property accounts by property from the start - backtracking after a year or so is a bookkeeping nightmare.

Keeping Good Financial Records

Keeping good financial records from the start of a property business is vital. Failing to keep track of income and expenses is likely to lead to paperwork spiralling out of control.

Landlords can also face unnecessary fines and penalties for failing to keep good business records and making mistakes on tax returns. Worst of all, poor records can lead to paying too little or too much tax.

The records to keep vary from landlord to landlord, but the basics should cover:

- Tenancy agreements

- Rent books

- Bank statements - including a separate account for your property business

- Receipts and bills for business expenses

- Business mileage records

- Finance statements for mortgages, credit cards or loans

Remember to tag each piece of paper.

Allocating Rent And Expenses To Tax Years

Always account for rent and expenses in the right tax year.

If they run across two tax years, share the cost between the years.

For example, buildings insurance costs £180 and runs from January 1 to December 31, crossing two tax years.

The cost is apportioned between January to March (3 months = 3/12 of the expense or £180/12*3 = £45) and April to December (9 months = 9/12 of the expense or £180/12* 9 = £135 or £180 - £45 = £135).

Calculating taxable profit or loss from letting property

Working out the figures is straightforward - you just subtract expenses from income.

The trick is knowing what is allowed as a property business expense as HMRC does not publish a list to help.

Here are some examples of some regular income and expenses for rental accounts:

- Rental income

- Any rent charged and received

- Any extra services charged separately, like meals, laundry or cleaning

Add up the total rental income for the year, and now look at allowable property business expenses. This list is not exhaustive but covers most of the common expenses charged by most landlords:

- Professional fees, like letting agents, your accountant and legal fees - but not the costs related to buying or selling a property

- Buildings and contents insurance or rent guarantee insurance

- Property business interest - on mortgages, credit cards or loans

- Maintenance and repairs

- Utility bills, like gas, water and electricity

- Rent, ground rent and service charges

- Council Tax

- Advertising

- Other business costs, like home as office, phone calls and using your car for business

Take the total for income and subtract allowable expenses to leave the net rental profit for the year. Next, deduct any allowances from the net profit, like 10% wear-and-tear or the renewals allowance if you let a furnished property. The remaining figure is the taxable profit or loss.

Dealing With Rental Losses

Property losses can be carried forward for setting off against future profits. A tax return has a section for noting losses. If losses are brought forward from a previous tax year, they must be deducted in full to leave the taxable amount. If they are more than the profit, the balance is carried forward to the next tax year with profits.

For example, a landlord made a £2,500 loss in 2010 and a £1,500 profit in 2011. The losses brought forward cancel the 2011 profits and £1,000 of losses is carried forward to 2012.

In 2012, the landlord makes a loss of £500, so £1,500 is carried forward to 2013. In 2013, the landlord makes a £2,000 profit, so the £1,500 loss is deducted, leaving £500 taxable profits. A taxpayer cannot opt to when to use losses - they must be deducted pound for pound against the first available profit.

If property ownership is shared, each owner has to declare their share of any profits or losses. To arrive at the figures, simply divide the income and expenses pro rata shares of ownership. For example, for two 50:50 owners, just divide the figures in half.

How Long Do You Need To Keep The Records?

Keep financial records for six years after the tax year to which they apply has ended.

Do not dispose of them even if you do not make a tax return, because you must produce them if asked by the tax man.

Appendix A
UK University Cities

The university cities are arranged in alphabetical order by country - England, Scotland and Wales.

The number of students is split as follows:

- UK - students from England, Scotland or Wales

- EU - students from the European Union, excluding the UK

- Other - students from outside the UK and EU

    Source: Higher education Statistics Agency (HESA) 2013

Appendix A - UK University Cities

ENGLAND		Number of students			
City	University	UK	EU	Other	Total
Bath	Bath Spa University	8330	110	110	8550
	The University of Bath	10725	1435	2975	15135
Bedford	Cranfield University	2415	1350	1475	5240
Birmingham	Aston University	7220	760	2225	10205
	Birmingham City University	20270	680	2215	23165
	Newman University College	3100	50	0	3150
	The University of Birmingham	24440	1290	5340	31070
	University College Birmingham	3595	515	875	4985
Bolton	The University of Bolton	7635	220	630	8485
Bournemouth	Bournemouth University	17210	850	1685	19745
	Arts University College	2540	130	195	2865
Bradford	The University of Bradford	11445	1040	1725	14210
Brighton	The University of Brighton	19160	1450	1465	22075
	The University of Sussex	9505	1000	2630	13135
Bristol	The University of Bristol	14900	960	3290	19150
	University of the West of England	27565	830	1995	30390
Buckingham	The University of Buckingham	940	190	765	1895
Cambridge	Anglia Ruskin University	18295	1330	1975	21600
	The University of Cambridge	13845	2265	3835	19945
Canterbury	Canterbury Christ Church University	17675	1000	435	19110
	University for the Creative Arts	5115	435	205	5755
Carlisle	University of Cumbria	10410	220	75	10705
Chelmsford	Writtle College	915	45	60	1020
Cheltenham	University of Gloucestershire	8350	205	520	9075
Chester	University of Chester	14785	175	250	15210
Chichester	The University of Chichester	5500	60	80	5640

Appendix A - UK University Cities

ENGLAND		Number of students			
City	University	UK	EU	Other	Total
Cirencester	Royal Agricultural College	1035	35	120	1190
Colchester	The University of Essex	10620	1925	2670	15215
Coventry	Coventry University	24630	1915	4505	31050
Derby	University of Derby	17090	570	835	18495
Durham	University of Durham	12850	880	2840	16570
Edgmond	Harper Adams University College	6120	125	155	6400
Exeter	The University of Exeter	13715	945	4060	18720
Falmouth	University College Falmouth	3670	100	90	3860
Guildford	The University of Surrey	10450	1465	3145	15060
Hatfield	University of Hertfordshire	22040	860	4330	27230
High Wycombe	Buckinghamshire New University	8865	455	450	9770
Huddersfield	The University of Huddersfield	19660	835	1845	22340
Hull	The University of Hull	19340	925	3045	23310
Ipswich	University Campus Suffolk	5745	70	35	5850
Keele	The University of Keele	9010	235	1415	10660
Lancaster	The University of Lancaster	9410	1130	2535	13075
Leeds	Leeds College of Art(#7)	1150	15	10	1175
	Leeds Metropolitan University	25515	870	1600	27985
	Leeds Trinity University College	3080	20	215	3315
	The University of Leeds	26720	1235	4560	32515
Leicester	De Montfort University	19220	720	1850	21790
	The University of Leicester	12680	865	3515	17060
Lincoln	Bishop Grosseteste University College	2230	0	30	2260
Lincoln	The University of Lincoln	12220	350	545	13115
Liverpool	Liverpool Hope University	7205	190	350	7745
	Liverpool John Moores University	21635	610	2210	24455

Appendix A - UK University Cities

ENGLAND		Number of students			
City	University	UK	EU	Other	Total
Liverpool	Liverpool Institute for Performing Arts	540	25	140	705
	The University of Liverpool	17265	620	3990	21875
London	Birkbeck College	17750	1010	820	19580
	Brunel University	11300	955	3625	15880
	Central School of Speech and Drama	760	85	145	990
	Conservatoire for Dance and Drama	900	195	155	1250
	Courtauld Institute of Art	290	60	85	435
	Goldsmiths College	6375	885	1200	8460
	Guildhall School of Music and Drama	545	160	95	800
	Heythrop College	945	25	75	1045
	Imperial College	9370	2365	4265	16000
	Institute of Education	5195	380	685	6260
	King's College London	19805	2515	4145	26465
	Kingston University	21655	1780	2615	26050
	London Business School	530	335	1215	2080
	London Metropolitan University	17845	2420	3015	23280
	London School of Economics	3260	1885	4655	9800
	Hygiene & Tropical Medicine School	630	130	485	1245
	London South Bank University	21295	735	1320	23350
	Middlesex University	17760	2150	3630	23540
	Queen Mary and Westfield College	10640	1285	2935	14860
	Ravensbourne	1435	50	110	1595
	Roehampton University	8105	435	710	9250
	Rose Bruford College	775	35	40	850
	Royal Academy of Music	430	145	185	760
	Royal College of Art	695	340	280	1315
	Royal College of Music	365	165	190	720

Appendix A - UK University Cities

ENGLAND		Number of students			
City	University	UK	EU	Other	Total
London	Royal Holloway and Bedford College	6740	1060	2065	9865
	Royal Northern College of Music	605	80	135	820
	St George's Hospital Medical School	4880	110	125	5115
	St Mary's University College	4730	230	120	5080
	The City University	11825	2480	5035	19340
	The Institute of Cancer Research	265	10	15	290
	The Royal Veterinary College	1845	75	195	2115
	School of Oriental and African Studies	2890	870	1645	5405
	The School of Pharmacy	1155	65	225	1445
	The University of East London	19305	1155	2760	23220
	The University of Greenwich	21245	1025	4170	26440
	The University of Kent	15805	1630	2875	20310
	The University of Warwick	18650	2195	6590	27435
	The University of West London	9965	835	1600	12400
	The University of Westminster	16080	2250	3170	21500
	Trinity Laban Conservatoire	670	155	90	915
	University College London	15445	3175	6905	25525
	University of London	255	70	120	445
	University of the Arts, London	10195	2230	4880	17305
Loughborough	Loughborough University	12680	825	2515	16020
Luton	University of Bedfordshire	15725	755	5795	22275
Manchester	Manchester Metropolitan University	31800	1115	1515	34430
	The University of Manchester	29450	2415	8815	40680
	The University of Salford	18265	1410	2080	21755
Middlesbrough	Teesside University	25900	380	1705	27985
Newcastle	The University of Newcastle	15555	1165	4335	21055
	The University of Northumbria	25415	580	3300	29295

Appendix A - UK University Cities

ENGLAND		Number of students			
City	University	UK	EU	Other	Total
Northampton	The University of Northampton	12935	210	1460	14605
Norwich	Norwich University College of the Arts	1570	40	25	1635
	The University of East Anglia	13715	750	3140	17605
Nottingham	The Nottingham Trent University	25260	615	2060	27935
	The University of Nottingham	26645	1895	7085	35625
Ormskirk	Edge Hill University	22075	190	85	22350
Oxford	Oxford Brookes University	15130	1160	2135	18425
	The University of Oxford	18540	2250	4800	25590
Plymouth	The University of Plymouth	27970	1280	1855	31105
	University College Plymouth	2710	20	120	2850
Portsmouth	The University of Portsmouth	19795	1175	2735	23705
Preston	The University of Central Lancashire	28465	915	2145	31525
Reading	The University of Reading	10405	845	2260	13510
Sheffield	Sheffield Hallam University	32550	555	4060	37165
	The University of Sheffield	19430	1220	5310	25960
Southampton	Southampton Solent University	10730	880	920	12530
	The University of Southampton	18185	1570	4380	24135
Stafford	Staffordshire University	20130	605	1030	21765
Sunderland	The University of Sunderland	13705	750	2925	17380
Winchester	The University of Winchester	5865	80	385	6330
Wolverhampton	The University of Wolverhampton	18895	955	1660	21510
Worcester	The University of Worcester	9890	505	300	10695
York	The University of York	13155	1055	3195	17405
	York St John University	5655	65	255	5975

Appendix A - UK University Cities

SCOTLAND		Number of students			
City	University	UK	EU	Other	Total
Aberdeen	SRUC	930	50	10	990
	The Robert Gordon University	9900	1010	1785	12695
	The University of Aberdeen	11600	2235	1680	15515
Dundee	The University of Dundee	13635	1175	1685	16495
	University of Abertay Dundee	4125	555	250	4930
Edinburgh	Edinburgh Napier University	10890	1675	1500	14065
	Heriot-Watt University	7070	1195	2605	10870
	Queen Margaret University, Edinburgh	4165	535	545	5245
	The University of Edinburgh	18880	3005	5785	27670
Glasgow	Glasgow Caledonian University	14090	475	1560	16125
	Glasgow School of Art	1225	145	350	1720
	Royal Conservatoire of Scotland	700	70	125	895
	The University of Glasgow	21060	2130	3105	26295
	The University of Strathclyde	16940	850	1965	19755
Inverness	University of the Highlands and Islands	6920	95	205	7220
Paisley	The University of the West of Scotland	14005	405	435	14845
St Andrew's	The University of St Andrews	5390	1315	3155	9860
Stirling	The University of Stirling	8820	540	1765	11125

Appendix A - UK University Cities

WALES		Number of students			
City	University	UK	EU	Other	Total
Aberystwyth	Aberystwyth University	9855	1075	775	11705
Bangor	Bangor University	9215	450	1590	11255
Cardiff	Cardiff Metropolitan University	8925	305	3780	13010
	Cardiff University	22440	1070	4235	27745
	University of Glamorgan	17800	870	2520	21190
Lampeter	University of Wales Trinity Saint David	5440	140	560	6140
Newport	The University of Wales, Newport	9000	225	760	9985
Swansea	Swansea Metropolitan University	5155	155	545	5855
	Swansea University	12600	365	1805	14770
Wrexham	Glyndwr University	5480	1370	2685	9535

Appendix B
Student Landlord Toolkit

These pages include template forms and letters mentioned in this book. They are free to use - and customise the forms to suit your personal requirements:

- Telephone card
- Viewing card
- Rental application
- Tenancy violation letter
- Notice to vacate
- Deposit assignment and release agreement
- Deposit account form

Telephone Card

A telephone card is a prompt for asking each prospective tenant the same questions when they call in response to an advert.

The intention is to make sure you have the relevant contact information; can analyse return on marketing spend and keep details of viewing appointments. The card should be cross-matched with a viewing card.

TELEPHONE INQUIRY	
Name:	
Time and date of call:	
Address (including postcode):	
Contact number:	
Email:	
Property inquiry source:	
University:	
Move in date:	
Viewing appointment:	Yes|No
Parking required:	Yes|No
Notes:	

Viewing Card

A viewing card holds the details of every prospective tenant who looked at your property. The card is a place to keep feedback - like questions asked, your impressions of the tenant and any follow-up action.

Check out the viewing cards for common queries - like how fast is the broadband or where the nearest supermarket is located. Add the answers to your property information sheet handed to prospective tenants.

VIEWING CARD	
Name:	
Time and date of viewing:	
Viewing type:	First\Return
Property shown:	
Quoted rent:	£
Quoted deposit:	£
Viewer's comments:	
Notes:	
Holding deposit:	£
Rental application completed:	Yes\No

Rental Application

RENTAL APPLICATION - PERSONAL DETAILS	
Last name:	
First names:	
Date of birth:	
Nationality:	
National Insurance Number:	
Driving licence number:	
Passport number:	
Current address:	
Type of tenancy:	Owned\rented\Living with parents etc
Landlord contact details:	

Do you have any county court judgements? Yes\No
If yes, please give details: (Date, Court, Creditor, Amount, Whether paid)
Have you ever been declared bankrupt? Yes\No
If yes, please give details:
Have you ever been evicted or asked to vacate a property?
If yes, please give details:
Have you ever lost a deposit or been sued for damage to a rental property?
If yes, please give details:

RENTAL APPLICATION - EMPLOYMENT	
Please give employment details for the past three years:	

CURRENT EMPLOYER

Name:	
Address:	
Job title:	
Date employment started:	
Gross salary:	

Previous employers

Name:	
Address:	
Job title:	
Start date:	
Leaving date:	
Gross salary:	
Reason for leaving:	

Name:	
Address:	
Job title:	
Start date:	
Leaving date:	
Gross salary:	
Reason for leaving:	

RENTAL APPLICATION - RESIDENCE	
If you have lived at your current address for fewer than three years, please give details of any other addresses during that time:	
Address:	
Type of tenancy:	Rented\Owner\Living with someone
If rented, landlord or letting agent contact details:	
Date moved in:	
Date moved out:	
Reason for leaving:	
Address:	
Type of tenancy:	Rented\Owner\Living with someone
If rented, landlord or letting agent contact details:	
Date moved in:	
Date moved out:	
Reason for leaving:	

RENTAL APPLICATION - DECLARATION	
I certify that the information I have provided in support of this rental application is correct. I understand this application will be denied if false information is provided. I give permission for the landlord or his agent to obtain a credit report based on the information I have provided.	
Signed:	
Print name:	
Date:	

Assigning And Releasing Deposits

If you let a student house on a joint tenancy, where a number of tenants have contributed to a single deposit, the chances are that someone will leave during the rental period.

The departing tenant will often try to claim a share of the deposit back, but you should keep all the deposit until the end of the agreement.

The tenants need to resolve these issues themselves if anyone moves out early. As belt and braces cover, ask the outgoing tenant to complete the deposit assignment form to cover you for any liability.

DEPOSIT ASISGNMENT AND RELEASE	
Date:	
Tenant:	
Landlord:	
Property address:	
The tenant named above agrees to assign any right or claim for the deposit held by the landlord in relation to the above property. The tenant also agrees to waive any right or claim to this deposit.	
Signed:	
Print name:	

Accounting For Deposits

This form clearly explains any deductions from a tenant's deposit, and should be handed over with the balance within 30 days of the tenant vacating the property.

The deposit form is a summary. Attached to the form should be a sheet for every category with a figure completed on the form. For instance, if cleaning came to £150, then a Sheet G should be attached with a copy of the receipt for the work carried out.

These working sheets give the tenant a breakdown for every penny of the deduction.

At the end, after adding up the credits (money in) and deducting debits (money out), a balancing figure is left. A negative balance means the tenant owes the landlord money, a positive balance means the landlord owes money to the tenant.

DEPOSIT ACCOUNT		
Date:		
To:		
Address:		
A Deposit received:	£	
B Interest rec'd (if any):	£	
C TOTAL CREDIT (A + B);		£
D Rent arrears:	£	
E Court costs:	£	
F Damage and repairs:	£	
G Cleaning:	£	
H Other deductions:	£	
I TOTAL DEBITS (A to H):		£
BALANCE (C- I):		£
COMMENTS:		

Tenancy Agreement Violation Letter

A template letter to send tenants who break the terms of a tenancy agreement.

TENANCY AGREEMENT VIOLATION	
Date:	
To:	
Address:	

This is a formal reminder that the terms of our tenancy agreement do not allow:

It has been brought to our attention that recently you have broken this term of our tenancy agreement by:

To comply with the terms and conditions of your tenancy agreement, you should:

I\we regret that failure to comply with the terms of the tenancy agreement can lead to eviction proceedings.

If you have any queries about this letter or wish to clarify the terms of your tenancy agreement, please feel free to contact me\us.

Yours sincerely

Owner

Tenant's Notice To Vacate

Tenants often do not follow the correct legal procedures or fail to give the information a landlord needs to know when they plan to leave a rental home.

This template collects all the information a landlord needs - and some feedback about the property and services provided.

Put a copy of this letter in the tenant's welcome pack and explainto them that filling in the details when they want to leave will help you and them work out a schedule within the terms of the tenancy agreement.

Each tenant should complete a form, as one may move out during the course of the tenancy while another wants to stay on.

NOTICE TO VACATE

Date:	

Address:	

This is to notify you that:

(PRINT TENANT'S NAME)

Hereby gives notice that he\she intends to vacate the property on:

(PRINT DATE)

I understand I am responsible for paying rent to the end of the agreement\the end of the notice period\until another tenant approved by the landlord has moved in and started paying rent.

Reason for moving:

Yours sincerely

Tenant

Appendix C
Online Resources

A list of useful online resources for landlords - most of these organisations offer free and impartial advice, but some are commercial.

Beware of forums - they can offer great advice to uncertain landlords, but some information is out-of-date and although forum posters are well-meaning, they sometimes offer incorrect information.

Accommodation For Students

The UK's leading student accommodation website.

www.accommodationforstudents.com

ARLA (Association of Residential Letting Agents)

The organisation representing around a third of the UK's letting agents

http://www.arla.co.uk/

CallCredit

The UK's third largest credit reference agency

http://www.callcredit.co.uk/

CB Richard Ellis (CBRE)

Property consultants who publish a quarterly student report

http://www.cbre.co.uk/

Communities and Local Government Department (CLG)

Government department that deals with housing and planning

http://www.communities.gov.uk/

Council of Mortgage Lenders (CML)

The trade body of all the UK's main bank and building society mortgage lenders

http://www.cml.org.uk/

Deposit Protection Service

One of the three government approved deposit protection services

http://www.depositprotection.com/

GovUK

Information about resolving landlord and tenant issues

https://www.gov.uk/browse/housing/landlords

Endsleigh

An insurance company specialising in landlord and tenant cover

http://www.endsleigh.co.uk/

Equifax

The UK's second largest credit referencing agency

http://www.equifax.co.uk/

Experian

The UK's first largest credit referencing agency

http://www.experian.co.uk/

Higher Education Statistics Agency

The latest facts and figures about UK universities and student numbers

http://www.hesa.ac.uk/

HM Revenue and Customs

Online property tax services and reference information for landlords

http://www.hmrc.gov.uk

Homelet

An insurance company specialising in landlord and tenant cover

http://www.homelet.co.uk/landlords/why-homelet

Knight Frank

Property consultants who publish an annual student report

http://my.knightfrank.com/research/

Landlord Law

A popular landlord resource run by solicitor Tessa Shepperson

http://www.landlordlaw.co.uk/home-page

LandlordZone

A free information resource for landlords

http://www.landlordzone.co.uk

Land Registry

Official online statistics about UK property

http://www.landregistry.gov.uk/

Landlord Moneysaving

The author's website offering moneysaving hints and tips for landlords

http://www.landlordmoneysaving.com

Lloyds Banking Group

Lloyds publishes an annual student property survey

http://www.lloydstsb.com

MyDeposit

One of the three government approved deposit protection services

http://www.mydeposits.co.uk/

National Approved Letting Scheme

Accreditation for landlords and letting agents

http://www.nalscheme.co.uk/

National Landlords Association (NLA)

A membership group for private residential landlords

http://www.landlords.org.uk/

Office of National Statistics (ONS)

Housing, census and other official public data

http://www.ons.gov.uk/

Residential Landlords Association (RLA)

A membership group for private residential landlords

http://www.rla.org.uk/

Royal Institution of Chartered Surveyors (RICS)

Membership body for chartered surveyors, valuers and estate agents

http://www.rics.org/

SafeAgent

Money protection scheme for letting agents

http://www.safeagents.co.uk/

Savills

Property consultants who publish an annual student report

http://www.savills.co.uk/

The Dispute Service

One of the three government approved deposit protection services

http://www.thedisputeservice.co.uk/

Lightning Source UK Ltd.
Milton Keynes UK
UKOW05f0244171013

219155UK00001B/29/P